Bible Lore and the Eternal Flame

Nihil obstat

Rev. Lawrence C. Brennan, S.Th.D
Censor
October 22, 2021

Imprimatur

Most Rev. James R. Golka
Bishop of Colorado Springs
October 22, 2021

+ James R. Golka

Most Reverend James R. Golka
Bishop of Colorado Springs

Bible Lore and the Eternal Flame

A numismatic, historical, and archaeological trip through Biblical times

Kenneth Bressett

Foreword by David Hendin

Whitman Publishing, LLC
PUBLISHING SINCE 1934
Whitman.com

Bible Lore and the Eternal Flame

Whitman Publishing, LLC
PUBLISHING SINCE 1934
Whitman.com

1974 Chandalar Drive, Suite D, Pelham AL 35124
ISBN: 0794849768
Printed in China

Select portions of this book were originally published in *Money of the Bible* (2013, third edition) by Kenneth Bressett.

Correspondence concerning this book may be directed to Whitman Publishing,
Attn: Bible Lore, at the address above.

WHITMAN®

Contents

Foreword

Ken Bressett is one of the grandmasters of numismatics. He has thrilled oh-so-many people through his passion for telling stories that help us understand our own histories through the study of coins. I have had the pleasure of knowing Ken for around 40 years, and his fascination with coins and their stories is clearly infectious to all of his many readers and friends.

In *Bible Lore and the Eternal Flame*, Ken narrates the Greatest Story Ever Told by taking readers on a journey of facts and artifacts going back several millennia, to trace the origins of our Judeo-Christian traditions.

As usual, Ken fills a gaping need by unabashedly presenting a narrative for beginners in the study of coins or other small remnants from ancient civilizations. At the same time, if the reader is more experienced, Ken provides plenty of rewards. He is a teacher, a motivator, and a preacher of the numerous positive aspects of the study of coins and other artifacts that link the modern reader to history.

One need not be religious or even agree that the Bible is a divine text to fully appreciate the thrill of reading Ken's narratives and seeing the excellent photographs of the objects being discussed. Ken reminds me very much of my late dad, also a numismatist, when he writes, "Knowing that genuine artifacts still exist provides a gateway to strengthening one's faith and provides a tangible connection to the past that can only be experienced through studying or actually seeing some of these interesting items. They are the closest thing to 'time travel' that one can ever experience."

Ken talks about the invention of writing and shows us examples of the earliest clay tablets with cuneiform letters. In his specialty of numismatics, he discusses trade and commerce from the earliest forms of barter through the precious metal economy, and into the age of coins in which we still live. Many readers will realize the actual connection between money and writing—the earliest writing was used to keep accurate records of financial transactions and accounts! Coins emerged more than a millennium later than the invention of writing.

Was Jesus a pioneer scholar of numismatics? Perhaps, since he shows us his own interest in money—16 of the 40 parables refer to coins or money, and "the topic is mentioned throughout the scriptures more than almost any other subject," Ken explains.

Ken uses examples of coins of the ancient world, and the stories related to them, to narrate the Judeo-Christian tradition from the invention of coinage right up to the Byzantine period. He begins his story in the days of the Old Testament, a time before coins existed, when "shekel" referred to a weight of metal, mainly silver. But, as the story reaches the "30 pieces of silver," Ken explains that NOW they are talking about coins—and he identifies them as silver shekels of Tyre. They portrayed a heathen god but were the purest of silver and truest of weight of their time, and they were the only coin accepted by the temple. Because Jews made pilgrimages to Jerusalem from around the ancient world, they arrived carrying only their local coins. These were converted into Tyre shekels or half-shekels by moneychangers near the Jerusalem Temple and, indeed, it was the behavior of these money changers that caused Jesus to disrupt their business by upturning their trading tables.

Through coins, readers reach the landmark when Rome accepted Christianity at the time of Constantine the Great (A.D. 307–337). Constantine had a dream before the battle of the Milvian Bridge in A.D. 312. In his dream, a flaming cross with the Latin words *In hoc signo vinces* ("By this sign you will conquer) appeared. "From that time forward, the Roman sun god was removed from Constantine's coins and replaced with non-religious depictions," Ken writes. Fascinating. I am betting that many professors of ancient history do not know this, because many historic details that are reflected in contemporary coins of the realm are often ignored except by specialists.

Ken also tells us that the face of Jesus does not appear on coins until the seventh-century reign of Justinian II. As for the origins of that image—well, Ken will tell the story better than I can here, so read on!

Many readers of this book will be surprised to learn that so many objects used around the time of Jesus still exist and can be seen in museums and private collections throughout the United States and the world. Ken not only tells us about these objects—from coins to oil lamps and ancient glass—but shows us photos of fascinating examples.

Indeed, each of these ancient objects is a portal to a continuum of human life across 4,000 years, an authentic key to the mind. Is every story true? We can never know. But Ken weaves tales that have been reconstructed by scholars since the Renaissance.

I found *Bible Lore and the Eternal Flame* to be a fun and fascinating book, and I'm delighted that **you** are reading it.

David Hendin

David Hendin, of New York, is the current Vice President and Adjunct Curator of the American Numismatic Society. He holds a bachelor's degree in education/biology and a master's degree in journalism from the University of Missouri, Columbia, and is a widely lauded expert in weights and currency of the ancient Levant, with a focus on Judaean, biblical, Roman provincial, and Nabataean numismatics. He is author of 18 books, including *Guide to Biblical Coins* (sixth edition, 2022); *Cultural Change: Jewish, Christian, and Islamic Coins of the Holy Land* (2011); and *Ancient Scale Weights and Pre-Coinage Currency of the Near East* (2007), along with numerous articles in scholarly journals.

Hendin is also a frequent speaker on Biblical numismatics and has lectured at University College, London; Nottingham University; American University, Beirut; University of Göthenberg, Sweden; Al Quds University, Jerusalem; Hebrew University; The Israel Museum; The Israel National Museum; Columbia University; and Yeshiva University, among others.

Publisher's Preface

In February 2021 the latest Kenneth Bressett manuscript, *A Penny Saved: R.S. Yeoman and His Remarkable Red Book*, was well into production. (The book debuted that August at the American Numismatic Association World's Fair of Money.) In the midst of that ongoing work, I mailed Ken an article that had caught my eye in the current issue of *Biblical Archaeology Review*. It was about specific uses of ancient pottery in the Holy Land. Years earlier Ken had shown me some Greek and Roman amphorae and coins from his personal collection, and I knew he'd find the article interesting.

A few days later he replied. "This subject is especially timely because lately I've been thinking about writing a sequel to my book *Money of the Bible*, and have been doing some research on related topics. I would appreciate your thoughts on this, and if you think it is worth pursuing . . ."

As any publisher would be, I was delighted by this proposal. And having been Ken's publisher for more than 15 years, I wasn't at all surprised that he was thinking ahead to his next project—even before the ink was dry on his latest book!

The resulting work, *Bible Lore and the Eternal Flame*, is not Whitman Publishing's first in the field of ancient coins. Recent publications include *Coins of the Bible* (Friedberg, 2004), *Money of the World: Coins That Made History* (Goldberg and Goldberg, editors, 2007), Harlan J. Berk's *100 Greatest Ancient Coins* (2008, with an expanded second edition in 2019), Paul D. Rynearson's *Collecting Ancient Greek Coins: A Guided Tour Featuring 25 Significant Types* (2008), and David MacDonald's *Overstruck Greek Coins: Studies in Greek Chronology and Monetary Theory* (2009).

Like Whitman, Ken Bressett is not a newcomer to the ancient world. Although he's popularly known as the longtime editor of the *Guide Book of United States Coins*, Ken has a long-held passion for ancient coins. In addition to his own research, in 1994 he crafted a new work combining two of Zander H. Klawans's well-established books (*Reading and Dating Roman Imperial Coins* and *An Outline of Ancient Greek Coins*) into a single volume. The resulting *Handbook of Ancient*

Greek and Roman Coins has since been a constant reference for collectors, with tens of thousands of copies in print. More recently, Ken's *Money of the Bible*, first published in 2005, has similarly proven to have evergreen appeal. It was updated with new editions in 2007 and 2013. Another Bressett opus, *Milestone Coins: A Pageant of the World's Most Significant and Popular Money* (2007), featured chapters on the ancient world and Biblical money.

Bible Lore and the Eternal Flame seeks to investigate the money of the ancient world as a means of exploring the Bible, and to bring students closer to understanding, and appreciating, the historical context of biblical stories.

This book is *not* a price guide, a market study, or a how-to handbook for collectors. What it offers students is that special magic of new light shone on enduring subjects; the clarity of obscure connections brought into sharp focus; and the pleasure of tales well told. These all are sparks that can lead to collecting. Or they may additionally inform and enrich the understanding of the historian, archaeologist, and student of theology or the ancient world.

Ken Bressett was careful to research this book from many disciplines and perspectives. He even sought the review of skeptics and non-believers, whose perceptions were given special consideration in parts of the manuscript. "I want to present a picture of how numismatics and archeology help in establishing a clearer image of ancient times," he told me in one conversation about the book. On the other side of the coin, it was important for Ken to seek the imprimatur of the Roman Catholic Church. After a careful review of the manuscript in accord with canon 827 of the Code of Canon Law, *Nihil Obstat* was issued and the Bishop of Colorado Springs granted the Church's imprimatur.

Many of the coins pictured herein are from Ken Bressett's personal collection. Reading *Bible Lore and the Eternal Flame* is nearly the equivalent of sitting down with one of the world's best numismatic storytellers and doing something Ken himself is always up to: learning, learning, learning, and enjoying every minute of it.

Dennis Tucker
Publisher, Whitman Publishing

Author's Preface

A journey of faith and illumination through numismatic and archaeological evidence

People from all walks of life find solace in reading passages from the Bible. Its popularity and allure extend to young and old alike. For many, it is a prime source of recorded knowledge about the world from the time of creation to the invention of the printing press. By its very nature, the text is considered sacred and beyond question by millions of faithful devotees. And there is additional satisfaction in knowing that structured research is able to provide factual evidence that can support the accuracy of biblical accounts, which are proven to be a trustworthy source of information.

Archaeologists have confirmed the historical accuracy of parts of the Bible by verifying many ancient sites, civilizations, and characters mentioned in biblical texts. Exploring Bible passages helps to illustrate and explain their meaning. Through numismatic and archaeological artifacts, it is also possible to once again see, touch, and better understand many of the items that were once used by our distant ancestors.

A modern-day view of life thousands of years ago is often clouded by anachronisms or conflicting images of wandering nomadic tribes, slaves being governed by Egyptian nobles, or persecution under harsh Roman rule. This ambiguity, often portrayed in popular movies and books, and a wish to learn more have prompted many to investigate any certifiable evidence that archeological finds have revealed over the centuries.

Published reports show that today there is no paucity of research and authentic artifacts to verify many of our favorite Bible stories. Consider yourself fortunate to live at a time somewhat compensating for the loss of knowledge through the destruction of the great Library in Alexandria, which was purported to have held as many as half a million scrolls at its peak, in the seventh century A.D.

Studying the Bible with a fresh insight and perspective has made me feel closer to the events and people of those ancient times by seeing first-hand that many of these artifacts still exist and can be viewed and examined in museum collections. It is comforting to realize how they explain and verify the Biblical stories we cherish. My hope is that you, too, will feel that same connection through the images that are presented here to illustrate, and describe, their role in history.

There is no contemporary written history of what the world was like when humans first walked upon the earth. By all accounts, even before the time of Adam and Eve, plants and animals must have existed to enable human beings to survive. The presence of other intelligent creatures prior to that time remains vague, but a dividing line is evident between primordial life and people who recognized that an almighty creator must have somehow provided this for their welfare. Ever since that time, cogent people everywhere have attempted to better understand, honor, and praise the beings they recognize as deities.

Your word is a lamp for my feet,
and a light onto my way.
(Psalms 119:105)

Introduction

NUMISMATICS *[noo məz'madiks]* is a study of currency that includes coins, tokens, paper money, and various other related objects. It is a subject that is of interest to coin collectors, researchers, students, and merchants, but in its purest form is a sub-discipline of archaeology similar to the investigation of materials related to commerce, including such things as pottery, jewelry, beads, metals, and barter items used by past civilizations. Studying these items has become a new source of interest and information for coin collectors who want to better understand how their treasured specimens relate to the economy and historical context of many diverse nations.

The instructive aspects of numismatics have intrigue me since 1937, when I first became aware of its potential as a teaching tool for better understanding of world history, art, and geography. Throughout the years I have researched and studied coins and trade items from various regions and time periods to provide evidence of their relation to historical events. A favorite area of examination has been linking ancient coinages to the people and events recorded in the Bible. In this endeavor, it is frequently possible to identify specific coins that are mentioned in Bible passages and better understand the meaning of those passages and their connections to actual usage of ancient forms of currency.

Traditional Biblical archaeology generally involves the study and history of Jewish and Christian peoples as recorded in the Old and New Testament and related contemporary references, such as the works of historian Flavius Josephus and the Dead Sea Scrolls. Classical archaeology includes a broader consideration of the ancient world, including the Mediterranean cultures of Greece, Rome, the Mycenaeans, and Minoans. Together, they explore the ever-fascinating world of antiquity.

A Hebrew scroll found in the caves of Qumran, Israel, near the Dead Sea.

The use of barter and trade items, as well as coins, after the eighth century B.C. was common to many cultures, and examples of such items still exist in museums and collections to confirm, and sometimes better explain, the authenticity of ancient history. Few resources are more detailed than the accounts found in sacred writings, and thus studying the Bible accounts of coins and money is a rewarding source of information and enjoyment for many coin enthusiasts. Most collectors refer to this special interest as "Coins of the Bible," or sometimes, "Money of the Bible."

A typical example of how the study of coins can aid in establishing the validity of their use in ancient times can be found in the account of the coin found in the fish's mouth (Matthew 17:24–27). This is the story of how Jesus told his disciple Peter to cast a line into the water and retrieve a fish that would contain a coin sufficient in value to pay the required temple tax for both of them.

The customary tax was used for temple repairs and other religious purposes, and it was required to be paid by all Jews wherever they lived throughout the ancient world. The annual tax was one-half shekel for every man over the age of 20 (Exodus 30:13–15).

Facts & Folklore

Silver tetradrachms, also called shekels, were the only foreign coins authorized for use by the Jews during Jesus's lifetime. This silver shekel of Tyre, dated year 28 (=98 B.C.), was used in circulation for decades.

The exact value, timing, and place of this event establishes precisely the kind of coin that must have been involved. By Jewish convention, it distinctly had to be a tetradrachm, called a shekel, from the neighboring city of Tyre. Such coins are still extant today and are regularly seen in museum exhibits, collections, or the coin trade. An account of this event is presented on page 120–121 of this book.

In my discussion of this and other similar events, there is no attempt to confirm or dispute any of the religious writings or teachings recorded in Bible passages. For many readers, these are a matter of faith or interpretation. Evidence can be provided by coins and other artifacts to establish certain facts, but these are not especially helpful for confirming traditional stories, parables, or beliefs that have been passed down through generations of faithful believers, until being recorded by learned people sometimes centuries after the actual events. Knowing that genuine artifacts still exist provides a gateway to strengthening one's faith and provides a tangible connection to the past that can only be experienced through studying or actually seeing some of these interesting items. They are the closest thing to "time travel" that one can ever experience.

When my family was young, in the early 1960s, I sought to demonstrate the use of ancient artifacts by showing how people lived in biblical times. A favorite discussion centered on the traditional Seder meal, and the similar Last Supper of Jesus. That always brought up the subject of the elusive Holy Grail, and its meaning. To establish that ordinary drinking cups and plates were used then as now, I showed my children examples of terracotta pieces that were used by common people at that time and place.

One particular cup that I find fascinating is of a style that would have been familiar to all of the 12 apostles sharing the meal. The one shown in this picture, or something very similar, would much more likely have been used than any of the elegant chalices made of gold, silver, or glass that are so often imagined.

Stories about the cup are omnipresent, as are numerous assertions about which is the original. Logically, some of the claims cannot all be true. Yet, it is possible to imagine the Grail based on the types of pottery and drinking vessels common at that precise time, place, and culture, giving us a fuller understanding of what everyday life was like centuries in the past.

There is no lack of information about such things. Learning about the past and people who lived centuries ago gives us a closer appreciation of how their efforts have impacted our lives. Hopefully, this brief glimpse of my personal interest in numismatics and archaeology will inspire you to dig deeper into the things you find of interest in world history, the daily lives of people past, and the Bible.

Through stories presented in *Bible Lore and the Eternal Flame*, Kenneth Bressett (with insight from longtime friends Robert Hoge, middle, and David Hendin, right) combines numismatics, anthropology, and archaeology to clarify customs, people, and life as it was in the Holy Land during biblical times.

Chapter 1

Genesis: The Story of Creation

"In the beginning, God created the heaven and the earth." (Genesis 1:1)

When it comes to the beginnings of the universe, science and religion are amazingly in accord. Essentially, there came a moment in time when a celestial force caused an event that formed the beginnings of everything we now know to exist. The details of exactly how and when that happened, as well as the actual nature of its architect, are of course areas where opinions begin to differ. Obviously, no human was there to witness or report on the event, and everything now known has come down to us through scientific study and divine revelation. For millennia before the invention of writing, the only means of preserving stories about the creation were through the spoken

words of those who sought to remember or understand the past, and the voice of God.

Over the centuries various cultures, religions, and languages have disseminated their individual interpretations, beliefs, ideals, and names for what scientists today call The Big Bang. Many of these explanations and descriptions of the beginning are similar and have been reported by religious leaders as having come to them in the form of dreams or direct messages from the one they know as God, Vishnu, Allah, Yahweh, or others.

The unfortunate and often confusing dilemma about the accuracy of these versions is confounded by being translated from one language to another, often across centuries. It is a situation that brings to mind the wisdom of Juliet in William Shakespeare's play, when she observes: "A rose by any other name would smell as sweet." In many cases, it is only a matter of what terms, descriptions, or words are used that cause the confusion. Some beliefs, like the world being carried on the back of a turtle, can hold special significance for their adherents, but aren't compatible with the consensus of scientific knowledge. Today we are blessed to be able to rely on the validity of words in the Bible not by faith alone, but together with confirmation by theologians, archeologists, scientists, and erudite research.

Reflections on the nature of the Supreme Being and the creation of the universe are mentioned here solely as a preface to understanding how viewing natural phenomena, and existing artifacts, can sometimes lead to a fuller knowledge and appreciation of the accounts and stories recorded in Judeo-Christian texts. In this book, the Supreme Being is referred to in communal English as "God," representing the equivalent of various Hebrew biblical names including Yahweh, as revealed directly to Moses, and Jesus Christ, as used in the Christian New Testament.

Jews and Christians alike believe that the first five books of the Old Testament, also known as the Written Torah and the Pentateuch, were written by a man known as Moses, who was inspired by God during the Hebrew Exodus from Egypt. The Book of Exodus places this event sometime nearly 4,500 years ago, though a lack of other historical evidence makes it hard for us to know today when and how

Oil lamps from the time of Moses and later.

the Exodus took place. The exact time when this and other portions of the Old Testament were first written is difficult to access because it covers a time period that extends roughly over 500 years. Obviously, it must have been inspired by a number of different people, and at different times, all sharing their vision of these epic events.

The book of Genesis contains some of the best-known Biblical references to the beginnings of mankind: Adam and Eve, The Garden of Eden, The Fall from Grace, The Great Flood, Methuselah, The Tower of Babel, and the descendants of Abraham. Through divine revelations and oral history, stories of these events have been passed down throughout the ages and later recorded in sacred writings.

The story of a Great Flood is told in Genesis, chapters 6:11–9:19. While there is scant scientific evidence of such an event, there is wide acceptance of a happening similar to that described in the Hebrew Torah and Christian Old Testament. Parallel narratives of a similar great flood can be found in earlier myths from Mesopotamia and Babylon. Other accounts and myths of great floods appear in cultures around the world, from Greece to India, China, and even various indigenous groups of the Americas.

Throughout most of these stories the theme is similar: the divine creator intends to flood the earth because of man's corruption but grants immunity to a savior, who can protect a chosen few by building a suitable vessel. In the Genesis narrative, Noah is instructed to

Noah's Ark, **Edward Hicks (1846).**

construct an ark in order to preserve his family and two of each animal. The waters eventually receded, and Yahweh granted redemption and sent a dove and rainbow as a sign of peace.

Greek mythology describes various great floods, and Plato mentions several in his writings. The ancient version closest to the Genesis story appeared in an eighth-century B.C. Babylonian copy of the "Epic of Gilgamesh." Even that, however, seems to have been preceded by a much older story found in the Sumerian creation myth, as recorded in tablets found in the ruins of Nippur, in modern-day Iraq, in the late 1890s. The oldest written story about the Great Flood comes to us from Ancient Samaria and was originally written on 12 clay tablets in cuneiform script. It is about the adventures of the historical King of Uruk, who lived somewhere between 2750 and 2500 B.C.

Eighteen years after many treasures were looted from the ancient city of Nippur, a clay tablet bearing the "Epic of Gilgamesh," re-

A portion of the clay tablets containing the "Epic of Gilgamesh," c. 1500 B.C.

garded as one of the world's oldest surviving pieces of literature, was returned to its place of origin. Iraq reclaimed more than 17,000 ancient artifacts looted and smuggled out of the country after the U.S. invasion in 2003. About 12,000 of the returned artifacts had been housed in the Museum of the Bible in Washington, D.C., and 5,381 had been held by Cornell University.

The history of the world is only well documented beginning with the invention of writing. Accounts are plentiful concerning Egyptian and Assyrian cultures. Other ancient texts refer to the Great Flood, Abraham, Moses, the Exodus from Egypt, and the Tower of Babel. An approximate timeline for events in Genesis is estimated in the following references:

Adam: 4000–3070 B.C. (Genesis 2:7; 5:5)
Methuselah: 3350–2350 B.C. (Genesis 5:21; 5:27)
Noah: 2950–2000 B.C. (Genesis 5:29; 9:29)
The Flood: 2350 B.C. (Genesis 6–9)
Tower of Babel: 2250 B.C. (Genesis 11:1–9)
Egypt founded: 2170 B.C.
Sodom and Gomorrah destroyed: 2065 B.C. (Genesis 19:1–29)
Abraham: 2165–1990 B.C. (Genesis 11:26; 25:8)

Unfortunately, there is little written evidence to chronicle the lives of prehistoric individuals other than kings and rulers. Many of the cities mentioned in Scripture no longer exist, and it is difficult to know with certainty when, where, or even if certain wars, civilizations, events, or catastrophes actually took place. The great museums of the world have exhibits and artifacts that support and explain ancient cultures, but the majority of people never get to experience any close connection with the distant past. One of the few hands-on activities that we can savor today is the study and collecting of ancient coins, pottery, and everyday items that have survived to give us a direct link and confirmation of past events.

Coins touched the lives of nearly everyone thousands of years ago, just as they do today. At a time when there were no other means of mass communication, coins served to spread the word about wars, kings, emperors, and current events. The images on ancient coins

Silver tetradrachm of Rhodes c. 229–205 B.C. The island of Rhodes was famous for its enormous Colossus statue, which overshadowed the harbor. A representation of the head of Helios the sun god, as seen on that statue, was used on many of the Rhodian coins of the third century B.C. for everyone to admire. It is the only remaining evidence of what the statue must have looked like. The rose on the reverse was a pun on the city name.

Silver tetradrachm of Roman Macedon, 148–147 B.C. This coin has the same basic design as that previously issued by the Macedonian republic but with the addition of a hand holding the olive branch of peace. It was issued to show the intent of a legate sent to Macedonia from Rome to quell the Andriscus revolt peacefully. The history of the world has often been recorded in coins of all times and cultures, often revealing little-known facts that might otherwise have been lost forever.

carried messages, or propaganda, intended to inform those who came in contact with them. As such, coins provide us with a running commentary on past events in a way that no other artifacts can. From the time that coins were first used as a medium of exchange, in the middle of the seventh century B.C., until the present, they have given us a nearly unbroken record of world history, boundary changes, rulers, and important events.

An 1873 H.H. Lloyd & Co. map showing Israel and surrounding areas as they were known in biblical times.

Chronological Overview of the Ancient World

- Pre-4000 B.C. Prehistoric times described in Genesis.
- 3000–2500 B.C. Noah. The Flood. Temple of Baal at Byblos.
- 2400–2200 B.C. Tower of Babel. Egyptian and Cretan culture.
- 2200–1950 B.C. Urbanization of mankind. Babylon founded.
- 2000–1730 B.C. Birth of Abraham, Isaac, and Jacob. Joseph sold into Egypt c. 1730.
- 1730–1550 B.C. Bondage in Egypt. Birth of Moses, his exile.
- 1550–1400 B.C. The Exodus. Death of Moses. Joshua and the Israelites invade Canaan.
- 1400–1300 B.C. Period of Judges. Eighteenth Dynasty of Egypt and age of King Tut and Nefertiti.
- 1300–1200 B.C. Trojan War. Oral tradition of Iliad and Odyssey. Treaty between Hittites and Egypt.
- 1200–1000 B.C. Saul made king. City of Jerusalem built by David c. 1000. Prophets Eli and Samuel.
- 1000–900 B.C. Kings David and Solomon of Israel. First Jewish Temple built c. 995.
- 900–800 B.C. Trade begins to flourish in Mediterranean and Near East. Prophets Elijah, Eliezer, and King Midas.
- 800–586 B.C. Jerusalem destroyed. Babylonian captivity c. 587. End of First Temple Period. Palace at Nimrud. Rome founded in 753. Age of Homer. First Olympics in Greece. First true coins minted in Lydia c. 630.
- 586–323 B.C. Daniel and Ezekiel. Persian King Cyrus captures Babylon. Jews return to Israel c. 536. Second Temple built c. 515. Darius and Xerxes rule Persia. Alexander the Great conquers Israel. Socrates. Use of coinage becomes widespread.
- 323–50 B.C. Palestine seized by Ptolemy, king of Egypt, then by Antiochus of Syria. Greek becomes the lingua franca. Maccabean revolt. Pompey of Rome annexes Israel as a province in 63. Roman and Judaean coinages begin. Punic Wars. Books of Maccabees and Dead Sea Scrolls written c. 100.
- 50 B.C–A.D. 1. Age of Julius Caesar, Cleopatra, Mark Antony, Herod, Pontius Pilate. Birth of Jesus of Nazareth. Augustus and Tiberius Caesar rule the Roman Empire.
- A.D. 1–350. Life of Jesus. The apostles. Nero. Rome burns. First and second revolt of the Jews. Temple in Jerusalem is destroyed. Masada. Bar Kokhba. Constantine the Great. Christian persecutions.
- A.D. 350–500. Talmud is completed. Old and New Testaments incorporated into the Bible. Byzantine Empire flourishes.

A Greek *ostracon*.

Chapter 2

When and How the Bible was Written

An inquiry into any aspect of the Bible must begin with an understanding of when and how this unique book was written. How did the stories originate? How have they come down to us across generations? And who recorded them? No single person wrote the Bible—not Moses, Abraham, the apostles, or even Jesus. It is a product of years of tradition, development, and painstaking selection of the divinely inspired works of many authors. Taken as a whole, the Bible is without doubt the greatest book ever compiled, one that touches on every aspect of humanity.

It has been said that writing is the most important of all inventions. That premise is difficult to refute when one considers what the written word has meant to civilizations throughout the world for millennia. We could never have developed into today's complex society without some system of writing and accounting, because communication and commerce depend on a method of recording that enables clear understanding between people and a permanent documentation of the many events and actions that have an impact upon our lives.

Prior to the invention of written records, most societies relied upon oral traditions and those who could preserve specific details by committing them to memory. The information was then passed from one generation to the next, but stories often suffered from loss of details and accuracy over time.

There is evidence that some of the earliest forms of physical recording were the use of stones or pebbles that were scribed with simple lines or marks, probably to indicate the quantity of some commodity or a measure of time. Incised stones dated to 8000 B.C. are thought to have been used to record a prehistoric transaction that must have involved the number of livestock being traded or sold. Similar tallying devices made of clay were employed by the Sumerians, a non-Semitic people who flourished in southern Mesopotamia around 3000 B.C., and were used to record inventories of farm products and other goods.

A Sumerian clay tablet, c. 2100 B.C. This was a typical receipt for produce inscribed in cuneiform writing. (Actual size approximately 38 mm.)

The Sumerian clay tokens made it possible for people to promise farm produce and other goods in payment of loans or taxes. Once the debts were paid, the tokens were destroyed, just as a modern check or bank draft is canceled when it clears an account. Archeological evidence indicates that these tokens were common throughout the Sumerian culture, and it was but a short advancement to the development of more complex writing on similar, but larger, clay tablets. Sometime around 3800 B.C., the script known as *cuneiform* evolved and replaced the crude markings on clay tokens. On these tablets, pictographic representations of abstract numbers recorded quantities and dates of transactions. The use of those clay tablet records soon evolved into the world's first writing system. The Sumerians are also credited with inventing the arch, the wheel, the division of the hour into 60 minutes, and numerous other important innovations.

An Assyrian cylinder seal with cuneiform writing.

Cuneiform script was written on soft clay with a wedge-shaped stylus that formed a long-lasting document. The most important of these clay tablets were baked. What began as a system of keeping property and other records soon became the means of recording historical events, of expressing poetry, stories, philosophies, religious ideas, and much more. The practice was later adopted by the Babylonians and spread throughout Mesopotamia. The Sumerian influence on the cuneiform system of recording is found in the writings of the great Semitic cultures that developed in the area, blending their cultures with the Sumerian culture and giving rise to some of the oldest accounts detailed in the Bible.

Evidence of writing on Babylonian clay tablets is not confined to a few isolated examples. The practice was widespread, and the thousands of clay records that are still extant are the source of much of our known history of the ancient world. Within the past century,

A Babylonian clay tablet, c. 2000 B.C., detailing the sale of sheep in an ancient transaction. (Actual size approximately 30 x 38 mm.)

many archaeological finds have provided a rich archive of records and correspondences detailing the daily lives of people who lived in the eighteenth century B.C.

Clay tablets have given us a better understanding of the origins of civilization in the lands between the Tigris and Euphrates rivers, including the early Semitic people. These records are especially important in the way they detail the development of trade, codes of law, and religion. From some of the translated cuneiform tablets, we know that the ancients paid debts in specified weights of silver or gold. The exchange unit of that time was called a shekel, which varied in standard weight over the centuries, but averaged about 8 to 10 grams.

The earliest known written complaint was recorded in cuneiform, around 1750 B.C. A customer wrote the complaint to a merchant named Ea-Nasir, who lived in the city of Ur, about the poor quality of the copper that he sold. This tablet is on display at the British Museum today.

The durability of the baked clay used for these ancient tablets is a stroke of good fortune for modern researchers, as the tablets are resistant to the ravages of time and their inscriptions can still be read with clarity. Many of the tablets that have survived seem to be as fresh as the day they were written nearly three thousand years ago. A cache that was unearthed in 1975 in excavations at Ebla, a city in what is now Syria, had been stored as a royal library or archive and contained more than 1,000 pieces that were stacked vertically on wooden shelves. One significant piece in the group recorded an interstate treaty, the oldest known in history, between Ebla and the city of Assur

The excavation site of the city of Ebla.

over the establishment of a free trade area. It included a variety of commercial and legal regulations, including some for crimes.

Other tablets in the Ebla discovery revealed an unknown language akin to the biblical Hebrew that was spoken more than 1,000 years later. One contained a vocabulary of Eblaite and Sumeric words, including an explanation in Eblaite of how the Sumeric words are pronounced.

OTHER FORMS OF ANCIENT WRITING

Unlike the Sumerians the Egyptians learned to use marsh-reed papyrus for a kind of paper that could be easily inscribed with a stylus and ink. At first they used a form of writing similar to cuneiform letters, but in time the ease of writing with paper and ink enabled them to create a more elaborate system. The Egyptians called their hieroglyphic script "the writing of the gods' words" or "sacred inscriptions." The notion that writing came from a god was widespread in the ancient world and may have formed the basis for some of the reverence that we hold today for the compilation of ancient writings known collectively as the Bible.

Hieroglyphic writing is inscribed on the Karnak Temple, surrounding illustrations of pharaohs and gods.

Ancient writing instruments, including papyrus, styluses, and scarabs.

Around 2000 B.C. Phoenicians in the city of Byblos (present-day Lebanon) devised an alphabetical script of some 80 signs. It was an unwieldy task for even the best scribe to use so many letters, and the system was soon abandoned in favor of the similar alphabetical cuneiform script of only 30 signs that was developed by the people of

Ebla. Although those scripts are unrelated to present-day alphabets, they influenced the development of the later Proto-Canaanite, Phoenician, Hebrew, early Greek, and Carthaginian (or Punic) alphabets. When Abraham went to Egypt, he followed the route of all other travelers, going north from Ur (which used cuneiform), up the Euphrates River and west to the north coastal region of Syria (which also used cuneiform), then south through Canaan, and west to his final destination, Egypt (which used hieroglyphics).

This silver shekel of Byblos under King Adramelek (375–351 B.C.) depicts a lion attacking a bull on the obverse, with the king's name in Phoenician letters above. A mythical hippocamp is shown on the reverse. The ancient city of Byblos was a major exporter of papyrus for the area, which was used for writing many documents, books, and holy works. In time, the word *byblos* came to mean book, and eventually it evolved into our word for the Holy Bible. (Actual size approximately 25 mm.)

By the twelfth century B.C., the Proto-Canaanite linear alphabet was developing into numerous scripts. To the East, it was the basis for Arabic and Ethiopic alphabets. In Canaan, it became the Phoenician, Hebrew, and Aramaic alphabets that recorded many of the early biblical accounts. Around 1100 B.C. the Greeks adopted the Phoenician alphabet for writing their non-Semitic language and added vowels. Our word "alphabet" comes from the Greek adaptation of the first two letters of the Semitic system that they borrowed: *alpha* and *beta*.

In addition to Egyptian papyrus, various other lightweight writing media were used, including wood, linen, leather, and parchment. They were usually inscribed with ink or paint, and while millions of such records must have been written, very few have survived because of the fragile nature of the material. Those that have come down to

us include sacred literature, contracts, wills, proverbs, tales, short stories, and all kinds of receipts. As with the clay tablets, many of them were originally stored in archives and libraries, but over the years, most have been lost.

The single most important find of such documents relating to biblical history was that of the incredible Dead Sea Scrolls treasure, unearthed in the ancient Judaean city of Qumran in the 1940s and 1950s. Archaeologists continue to explore the site, with new scrolls being discovered, along with remnants of food and clothing, as recently as 2021. The ongoing translation and analysis of the text preserved on these delicate scrolls is of the utmost importance to our understanding of the original biblical manuscripts.

Among the Dead Sea Scrolls, a sheet of copper had been inscribed. On this scroll were the instructions for finding the buried valuables of the community. Known as the "Treasure Scroll," it was made of copper to ensure its preservation and survival. It had been carefully set aside and hidden so that it would be preserved for generations. Unfortunately, the key to finding the treasure has never been discovered, if it still exists, and may remain a mystery until other pieces of the puzzle are unearthed.

Ancient inscriptions on metal were relatively common. Silver and gold plates have been found with text relating to the Assyrian King Sargon II (c. 721–705 B.C.), and Darius I of Persia (c. 522–486 B.C.). Metals used as writing materials had a special significance to ancient peoples and were often chosen for temple gifts and messages considered of the highest importance. One of the oldest is a Sumerian gold tablet found in Mesopotamia that has been dated to the third millennium B.C.

A fragment of a bronze military diploma, dated to A.D. 116, for an unknown horseman of cohort II Flavia Brittonum Equitata in Moesia Inferior (the modern-day Balkans), under the governorship of Q. Pompeius Falco, who commanded the Legio X Fretensis as propraetor of Judaea, c. 107–110. Falco served during the reign of Emperor Trajan and later became governor of Britain for Hadrian (c. A.D. 118–122). (Actual size approximately 55 x 60 mm.)

Nearly all of the ancients occasionally wrote on metal, but the Romans were perhaps the most prolific. The most famous metal plates in the ancient world, undoubtedly, were the 12 tablets of Roman law, which were erected in the forum of Rome in 450 B.C. In other instances, people, victories, and special events are known to have been commemorated with inscribed metal plates. Unfortunately, most of them have been melted over the years, and few have survived.

Roman soldiers were given their military discharge diplomas in the form of a copper plate to ensure that it would never be destroyed. It was proof of their honorable discharge and not only exempted them from further conscription, but entitled them to many privileges. Veterans were granted Roman citizenship and the right to a Roman marriage.

Stone was another choice for preserving important messages because its strength and durability far exceeded that of the clay tablets or the more fragile papyrus. Stone inscriptions were used extensively throughout Egypt on massive memorials and were considered particularly desirable for the perpetuation of codes of law and legal agreements, for immortalizing the deeds of rulers, and for many religious proclamations. A metal chisel and hammer were typically used to inscribe the local stones, particularly the soft Egyptian limestone. The Greeks and Romans preferred marble for stone inscriptions and used it almost exclusively. The oldest known stone inscription is a limestone tablet from Kish, Mesopotamia, dating to the fourth mil-

The Siloam pool at the end of Hezekiah's tunnel, outside the walls of the Old City of Jerusalem.

lennium B.C. Writing on stone was a widely known form of communication by the sixteenth century B.C. when Moses received the Ten Commandments from God.

> *And the Lord said to Moses: "Come up to me into the mount, and be there, and I will give thee tables of stone, and the law, and the commandments which I have written, that thou may teach them." (Exodus 24:12)*

One highly significant example of a stone inscription that was found in Jerusalem, and is still available, is a proclamation of King Hezekiah of Judah dating to the year 701 B.C. It describes in detail the design of the Siloam Tunnel being dug into the mountain. Not only does it show the great accuracy of the Bible, which records the battle with the Assyrian King Sennacherib (2 Kings 18) and the digging of the tunnel to divert water in advance of the Assyrian siege, but it also answers the question of the true location of Jerusalem before the Babylonian Captivity in 587 B.C., when the city was plundered and destroyed, including Solomon's Temple, and its residents were taken by force to Babylon.

An Akkadian cuneiform inscription on this clay tablet, c. 580 B.C., lists certain rations and mentions the name of Jeconiah (Jehoiachin), king of Judah, and the Babylonian captivity.

The Code of Babylonian King Hammurabi, one of the earliest known written legal directives, was inscribed on a stone monolith about 1750 B.C. It ordains the basis of both criminal and civil law and defines procedures for commerce and trade. The text is considered the predecessor of both Jewish and Islamic legal systems.

Unlike legal codes and the great achievements of kings and armies, everyday record-keeping often relied on the simplest materials available to ancient people. Broken potshards were a favorite medium for writing with paint or ink. The baked earthen material was strong, long lasting, and abundant. The broken pieces of clay pottery used for writing were called *ostraca*, and were sort of like today's scratch pads. They were

An ostracon or potshard, c. A.D. 400, with an ink inscription similar to the type of writing used to transcribe the Bible. (Actual size approximately 90 x 123 mm.)

used for short messages, school lessons, receipts, and even voting ballots. Ostraca were used in this way as early as the second millennium B.C., and probably as late as the sixth century A.D.

A piece discovered by archeologists in 1997 contains what may be the oldest non-biblical reference to King Solomon's Temple. It records a donation to the "House of Yahweh" and is estimated to be nearly 3,000 years old. Solomon's Temple was generally believed to have been built sometime in the tenth century B.C. It lasted for four centuries until it was destroyed by Babylonian soldiers. The Bible frequently refers to the Temple by the Hebrew term "the house of the Lord," but that term has been found complete in only one inscription other than the Bible. The ostracon inscription indicates a Judaean king, "Ashyahu," sent it as a request to a temple contributor, commanding a donation of three shekels of silver for "the House of Yahweh." This ostracon was apparently written to serve as a receipt for what would have been approximately one and a half ounces of silver, at a time before coins had been introduced.

The word "ostracize" comes from the practice in Athens of voting on banishment by writing an undesirable's name on a potshard. One of the most famous uses of ostraca was at the besieged fortress of Masada, where, according to Jewish historian Flavius Josephus, the choice of who would carry out the pact of death was decided by ten marked shards chosen by lot. Traditional accounts of the siege of Masada say that hundreds of Jewish resistance fighters suffered death by their own selected members rather than surrender to the Roman army.

The fortifications at Masada.

CONSTRUCTION OF THE BIBLE

The Bible is a collection of 66 books written by 40 inspired writers over a period of nearly 1,600 years. The original manuscripts that comprise this material have been translated into modern languages many times in efforts to make the books accessible to new audiences while still preserving the meaning as closely as possible to the Hebrew, Aramaic, Greek, and Latin texts. The scribes who copied and recopied the original scrolls were dedicated to accuracy and have provided reliable accounts of ancient testimony. Modern study and translations of the Dead Sea Scrolls also provide evidence for the reliability of Jewish Scriptures in the Old Testament, as do the extensive writings of the contemporary historian Flavius Josephus.

Although the Bible was written by many different authors, it is consistent in its messages and interpretations of past events, prophecy, poetry, and theology. Despite their complexity, differences in writing styles, and coverage of vast time periods, the books of the Bible agree well in theme and historical facts. Most of the ancient writings on fragile papyrus have long since vanished, yet many copies of very early Old Testament texts have been preserved in the Dead Sea Scrolls. Some of the known New Testament manuscripts date to within 24 years after Jesus's death.

In biblical and numismatic archeology, researchers try to bring together all known facts to help us understand the scriptures better, to evaluate critical questions, and to gain a fuller appreciation of the ancient world in which the Bible was written. Countless discoveries have furnished a deeper understanding of the meaning of parables. Coins of the Roman emperors and Jewish procurators provide evidence of their existence and corroboration of their historical roles in the Bible. It is here that science and religion come together to present a richer account of the ancient world that surrounded those people and places.

The association of coins with biblical references reaffirms that the Bible is not talking about unsubstantiated places and unverifiable events, but real people and places in history. Among the many examples that could be cited are the gold darics of King Darius, the Persian monarch who is mentioned in ancient texts dating to 498 B.C. and described in Ezra 4:6. Persian, Greek, and Roman coins, known as the daric, drachma, and denarius, are all mentioned in the Bible and can be clearly identified and verified by examples that are still extant today. Researchers and numismatists agree that archaeological discoveries have only reinforced many biblical references.

THE ETYMOLOGY OF BIBLE VERSES

The original passages that are included in the Bible were written at different times and in different languages. Some were written in Hebrew, while others were in Greek and still others in Aramaic. Almost all of the books of the Old Testament were originally written in Hebrew, with the exception of the second Book of Maccabees and the Book of Wisdom, which were written in Greek and are considered part of the Catholic deuterocanonical texts. Most scholars believe that the books of the New Testament were originally written in Greek, with possible early source texts or oral stories in Aramaic.

The Roman *Vulgate*, written by St. Jerome of Dalmatia in A.D. 382, was a translation into Latin from the original Old and New Testament languages. No English versions of the Bible were made until a thousand years later, in 1384, when the controversial Wycliffe Bible was published.

In the more modern translations of biblical writings, the King James Version uses words of Anglo-Saxon origin that were familiar to English readers in the seventeenth century. The Douay-Rheims Version freely uses words of Latin origin and Latinizes the names of some of the books.

In addition to the many translations, various church leaders have also gathered on several occasions—from Marcion of Sinope in A.D. 140, to the Council of Rome in A.D. 382, to the Council of Trent, the Thirty-Nine Articles, and the Synod of Jerusalem in the sixteenth and seventeenth centuries—to determine which books and texts should be considered part of biblical canon. This has led over time to divergences in the canons of different Christian faiths, with most Protestant Bibles containing 66 books, the Catholic Bible containing 73, and the Eastern Orthodox Bible containing 79.

Several versions of the Bible have been considered here in order to focus on the clear and precise meaning of Jesus's many parables that mention money. Sixteen of his 40 parables make reference to coins or money, and the topic is mentioned throughout the scriptures more than almost any other subject.

The Council of Trent.

Chapter 3

Trade and Commerce in Ancient Times

The world as we know it today could not function without a complex monetary system. From coins and paper currency to checks, credit cards, and bank drafts, money is involved in every life and every transaction, even if we seldom think about why this is our money, or why it is valued at the amount we believe it to be worth. There was, of course, a time when none of this existed, and the concept of using credit cards or cyber currency would have been as strange to primitive man as his world of trading seems to us today.

The transfer of goods from one person to another is as old as mankind and an important part of even the most primitive civilizations. A skillful toolmaker soon learned that it was to his advantage to trade his products to the hunters that could provide him with food. Cattle, grains, and ornamental beads were found to be desirable trade items in early prehistoric times. Those exchanges must have been measured only in the desirability and immediate needs of those who traded, and value quite likely varied from transaction to transaction. The concept of uniform values did not arise until there was accumulated wealth that could be stored in some form and traded, even for items deemed to be nonessential.

Wealth in the form of crops or livestock was the usual mark of a successful trader, but there was always the danger of loss by spoilage and sickness, plus the difficulties of moving livestock over long distances. It was also often impossible to barter sheep or cattle for items of a much lesser value. Consider the problem of making change for a lamb that might require half a chicken, two doves, and a small utensil. These difficulties soon required the use of a promissory agreement that could be repaid at a later date with an accumulation of goods. There was also the problem of establishing the relative values of bartered items between traders who might value those items differently.

Commodity money, which served civilization from the earliest of times, continues to be used in some societies up to the present day.

Even the current U.S. tax forms ask the question of value received in the form of barter. Much of Europe during a large part of the Middle Ages existed on a system of barter rather than a cash economy, and in colonial America "country pay" was the common, and usual, medium of exchange among rural people. For 3,000 years Egypt had no coins, and though ingots and rings of precious metals may have served the purposes of money in negotiations between kings and great merchants, money was practically unknown to the ordinary people.

In a well-developed and open economy, the use of money—that is to say, a commonly accepted medium of exchange—becomes indispensable. This money system must be widely accepted as being of stable value, recognizable, transportable, durable, and easily divisible. Over time the most useful metals (gold, silver, and copper) became popular choices, being the ideal media that could be used in nearly every transaction. Those precious metals have continued to serve this function well for thousands of years.

Money, as a medium for the exchange of goods, requires some understanding of "property," its use as a measurement of value, and some conception of the way in which both parties can benefit by exchange. These requirements were neither natural nor easy for primitive man, and the transition from trade and barter to the sophisticated use of coins and credit was a long and difficult passage. Over the ages, many things have served as money in different societies: hide-scrapers, beads, shells, stones, livestock, and tusks. In biblical lands, however, the evolution was generally quite straightforward, with precious metals almost always being the first choice as money of exchange that was nearly universally accepted.

The need for some convenient units of precious metal became widespread as trade expanded throughout the ancient world, and in time small lumps of gold and silver, or other metal items, became generally acceptable in trade. The metals that were used were not pure, but often combined with other metals as found in nature. The regular combination of gold and silver, known as electrum, was the most valuable prior to the advent of refining methods. Copper, or the alloy known as bronze, was valued because it was so useful in fabricating a multitude of utilitarian items.

Ancient electrum pre-coin money units were simple disks of metal with punch marks on one side and a rough anvil impression on the other.

Among the earliest known forms of metal for exchange are bronze ingots from the second millennium B.C., in the shape of cast fillets approximately 10 inches long and 2 inches wide. Similar silver and gold strips were apparently also used, and are known from hordes of small pieces that were cut from the strips. The Hebrew people during much of the Old Testament times measured this metal in the unit called a shekel. The term referred to a specific weight and was used to quantify many diverse commodities long before the beginning of coins. Quarter, half, and two-thirds shekel weights are frequently mentioned in the Old Testament, as in 1 Samuel 9:8: “Behold, I have here at hand the fourth part of a shekel of silver; that will I give to the man of God, to tell us our way.”

In addition to raw metals and ingots, fabricated items were also held to be of great value. All classes of people coveted jewelry and ornamental items such as rings, bracelets, chains, and earrings, which were as popular 4,000 years ago as they have been ever since. The first such mention of wealth in the Bible was in Genesis 13:2, where Abram (later called Abraham) is described as being “very rich in cattle, silver, and gold.” Abraham’s wealth is again mentioned in another passage from Genesis (24:1–38) that tells of how he sent his servant to find a wife for his son Isaac. Upon encountering Rebecca at the well, the servant gave to her a number of precious items to win her favor:

> *When the camels had finished drinking, the man took out a gold ring, a half shekel in weight, which he fashioned on her nose, and he put on her wrists two gold bracelets weighing ten shekels.*

He also said, in Genesis 24:34–35, 53:

I am Abraham's servant. The Lord has blessed my master abundantly so that he has become a rich man. He has given him flocks, herds, silver, gold, men and women servants, camels and asses.

The servant brought forth silver articles, and gold articles, and clothing, and he gave them to Rebecca; and to her brother and to her mother, precious things.

Jewelry in the form of bracelets and rings was commonly traded in the first millennium B.C. In Luristan (Iran), this copper bracelet, decorated with lion's head terminals, was a popular item. (Actual size approximately 62 mm.)

Golden earring or nose rings, like this one weighing 1/4 shekel, have been cherished jewelry for thousands of years. (Actual size approximately 17 mm.)

In ancient Egypt, large rings of precious metal were used as payment in place of coins. This gold ring with decorated ends is attributed to the second millennium B.C. (Actual size approximately 32 mm.)

In ancient Egypt, at the time of the stories told in Genesis, similar items were used as money and a store of value and wealth by the nobility. Common laborers and slaves had little use for money and were usually paid in grain and other necessities of life. Coins that came into use in the seventh century B.C. in other regions were not extensively used in Egypt until the Alexandrian era, in the fourth century. An early reference to the Egyptian concept of wealth is seen in Genesis 41:42:

> *Then the Pharaoh said to Joseph, "I give you charge of the whole land of Egypt." Taking the signet ring from his own hand, he put it on Joseph's. He dressed him in linen robes, and put a chain of gold around his neck.*

Details from a tomb in Thebes, c. 1400 B.C., show an Egyptian weighing large metal rings against lamb-shaped weights. Bronze rings similar to those in the paintings have been found in the region and are believed to be a form of trade currency from that time period, along with other rings of gold or silver. The very few Egyptian monetary gold rings that are still in existence are consistent in decoration and form but vary in size, and they would have been valued according to their weight. Gold earrings and bracelets that are prevalent

Ancient rings and gold earrings.

throughout the ancient world were decorative items that represented the wearer's wealth and status, but they could also be used as money whenever necessary. Gold clothing ornaments were also a popular form of adornment among the rich prior to a more convenient means of storing their money. In Exodus 32:2, Aaron said to the Israelites:

> *"Have your wives and sons and daughters take off the golden earrings they are wearing, and bring them to me."*

Then in Exodus 32:24:

> *And I said to them, "Who has gold?" They broke it off, and gave it to me, and I cast it into the fire and fashioned a molten calf.*

In the Book of Numbers (3:50) we read, "of the firstborn of the children of Israel Moses took the money, a thousand three hundred and sixty-five shekels, according to the shekel of the sanctuary." Job 42:11 contains the following passage: "everyone gave him a piece of money, and every one a golden ring." And in Jeremiah 32:9–10, it is written, "I bought of Hanameel, mine uncle's son, the field which is in Anathoth, and weighed him the money, seventeen shekels of silver. And I subscribed the writing, and sealed it, and took witnesses, and weighed the money in balances."

MONEY THAT REBUILT THE HOLY TEMPLE

In the kingdom of Judah, Solomon's Temple was the center of worship from the time it was built around 1000 B.C. until it was virtually destroyed by Nebuchadnezzar of Babylon when he captured the city of Jerusalem in 587 B.C. At that time its gold, bronze, and silver furnishings were taken to Babylon and held there for the next 50 years. When the Persian King Cyrus allowed the Jews to return from Babylon to Jerusalem in 538 B.C., he gave them permission to rebuild Solomon's Temple. He also returned some of the gold and silver objects that Nebuchadnezzar had taken from the temple. When Cyrus ordered the temple construction in Jerusalem, he also decreed that everyone should contribute their silver and gold to the rebuilding:

> *Let (the Israelites) go up to Jerusalem which is in Judea, and build the house of the Lord the God of Israel: he is the God that is in Jerusalem. And let all the rest in all places wheresoever they dwell, help him every man from his place, with silver and gold, and goods, and cattle, besides which they offer freely to the temple of God. (Ezra 1:6)*

Although this construction, which was completed in 515, was during a time when coined money was making its appearance, the Israelites were more accustomed to the Babylonian use of trade and bullion transactions. The book of 2 Kings 17:1–8 emphasizes that "the children walked in the ways of their Assyrian captors, and worshiped strange gods." As such, it would not have been unusual for the Jews to use Persian and other gold ornaments to adorn their clothing, and for them to have earrings, bracelets, and rings of precious metals. They must have used these items as "money" and trade items, just as they used the coins of the kings Cyrus and Darius in a somewhat later period.

Gold darics of Persia were the first coins mentioned in biblical literature. In 1 Chronicles 29:7, and later in Ezra 8:27, it is recorded that large sums of gold in the form of Persian daric coins were used to rebuild the Temple in Jerusalem.

And how he gave them the law that they should not forget the commandments of the Lord, and that they should not err in their minds, seeing the idols of gold and silver, and the ornaments of them. (2 Maccabees 2)

And the Lord said to Moses: Say to the children of Israel "Thou are a stiff-necked people; once I shall come up in the midst of thee, and shall destroy thee. Now presently lay aside thy ornaments, that I may know what to do with thee." So the children of Israel laid aside their ornaments by Mount Horeb. (Exodus 33:5–6)

Gold ornaments were fastened to clothing as decorations and often used as money when the need arose. This piece, in the form of a lamassu (a winged animal with a king's head), was made in the sixth century B.C. When Persian King Cyrus allowed the Jews to return to Jerusalem and rebuild their temple, they gave their ornaments to be melted and used to build the city and temple. A piece of this size and weight was equivalent to two Persian silver sigloi, or 1/16 of a gold shekel. (Actual size approximately 30 x 23 mm.)

Gold clothing ornaments (a Persian equivalent of buttons, with an eyelet on the back to be sewn onto clothing) were very likely among the items committed to the temple building fund. These were the pride of those who could afford to display their wealth and their allegiance to the Persians. They were often made in the form of "strange gods" that the Jews had come to accept. It is easy to imagine that hundreds of similar things went into the melting pot, along with the rings, bracelets, earrings, and vessels that filled several baskets. In 2 Kings 1 the passage states, "Ye daughters of Israel, weep over Saul, who clothed you with scarlet in delights, who gave ornaments of gold for your attire."

Some of the oldest silver coins were made on the island of Aegina where their famous silver "turtles" were used as bullion for international trade. Staters made as early as 525 B.C. show a sea turtle and segmented punch mark on the reverse. (Actual size approximately 20 mm.)

The famous "owls" of Athens circulated throughout the ancient world around the middle of the fifth century B.C., when this attractive early-style tetradrachm was created. (Actual size approximately 25 mm.)

Silver staters of Corinth circulated freely throughout the ancient world. They were known as "colts" because of the design showing Pegasus, the legendary horse that was stabled near the city. (Actual size approximately 22 mm.)

These, and hundreds of other similar passages in the Old Testament, describe the use of barter, trade, gold, silver, and other items of value that were used as a form of money in ancient times. Nowhere are coins actually mentioned in any place prior to their appearance in the seventh century B.C. The occasional use of coin-like terms in some early Bible quotations are always those of translators attempting to relate unfamiliar expressions with words that might be familiar to contemporary readers. The frequent use of the word "shekel," which was a weight, is a prime example of something that did not become a coin until the middle of the first century A.D.

Money of account, for which there was never a coin issued, is mentioned in a few biblical passages, but the talent has never been precisely valued. In terms of silver, it seems to have been 750 ounces,

3,000 shekels in gold, or 6,000 Greek drachmas. Fifteen talents of silver were equal to one talent of gold. The maneh, or mina, was equivalent to 50 or 60 shekels. In some translations, the word "sicle" is used instead of "shekel," as in Numbers 18:16: "and the redemption of it shall be after one month, for five sicles of silver, by weight of the sanctuary. A sicle hath twenty gerahs (obols)."

COINS IN THE OLD TESTAMENT

The earliest actual coins mentioned anywhere in the Bible are the gold darics of the Persian King Darius I, who ruled from 522 to 486 B.C. After 486, the successors to Darius issued similar gold darics and silver sigloi, with the image on one side of a bearded, kneeling archer holding a spear and bow, and an oblong incuse punch mark on the reverse. The daric is specifically identified in 1 Chronicles 29:6–8:

> *Then the heads of the families, the leaders of the tribes of Israel, the commanders of thousands of hundreds, and the overseers of the king's affairs came forward willingly and contributed for the service of the house of God five thousand talents and ten thousand darics of gold, ten thousand talents of silver, eighteen thousand talents of bronze, and one hundred thousand talents of iron.*

In Ezra 8:26–27, we read the following:

> *I consigned it to them in these amounts: silver, six hundred and fifty talents; silver utensils, one hundred; gold one hundred talents; twenty golden bowls valued at a thousand darics; two vases of excellent polished bronze, as precious as gold.*

Prior to the conquest of Lydia by the Persians, few coins were used by the Persian kings. As the kingdom expanded west, it found a need for the medium of exchange that had been implemented around 550 B.C. by King Croesus of Lydia, and his successors. In addition to being remembered for his legendary wealth, Croesus should be equally famous for his innovation of issuing corresponding coins that were made of nearly pure gold or nearly pure silver. Previously, coins were often made of a natural mixture of the two metals that is known as electrum (see page 30 for illustration). The difference in value between gold and silver was the influential factor in separating them into two distinct coins. Curiously, the design used on these early coins was often the same for both metals. The practice of using diverse coinage metals was continued by the Persians thereafter, and in other countries ever since.

A silver half stater of Lydia, 561–546 B.C., issued by King Croesus (who is still famous for his remarkable wealth). His coins were the first to be made of either silver or gold, rather than a mixture of the two metals. (Actual size approximately 17 mm.)

The knowledge of how to mint and use coins had spread to all of the important Greek cities around the Mediterranean area by the end of the sixth century B.C. Merchants from every part of the Greek world used coins in the exchange of goods. Not all communities minted their own coins, and many depended on the use of coinage from other districts. The Israelites had to wait several centuries before their economy and government was strong enough to support the responsibility of issuing their own coins. In the period prior to their independence, the Jews were often compelled to use the money of their subjugators and that of foreign lands, some of which they found offensive because the coins usually displayed graven images, often those of local gods. The reluctance of Jews to use heathen money was rooted in their adherence to the decree quoted in Exodus 20:1, 4, and 20:

> *Then God delivered all these commandments: "You shall not carve idols for yourselves in the shape of anything in the sky above or on the earth below or in the waters beneath the earth. Do not make anything to rank with me; neither gods of silver nor gods of gold shall you make for yourselves."*

Many other coins were made and used throughout the numerous districts mentioned in the Old and New Testaments. It seems likely that most of them would be familiar to those who handled large sums of money and needed to convert one weight system to another when making a transaction. The most commonplace would have been those pieces from the districts closest to Palestine, where the shekel and its fractions was a standard for many coins. Coins from Aradus, on the northern coast of Phoenicia, were popular from about 500 B.C. until the mid-first century B.C.

The city of Aradus in Phoenicia issued this silver drachma in 161 B.C. It could have circulated in Jerusalem just prior to the time the Jews were allowed to make coins of their own. (Actual size approximately 16 mm.)

Silver tetradrachms of Aradus were valued at one shekel each at the time this piece was made in 80 B.C. (Actual size approximately 28 mm.)

> *And when Moses had gathered the multitude together again, he ordained that they should offer half a shekel for every man, as an oblation to God; which shekel is a piece among the Hebrews, and is equal to four Athenian drachmae.* (The Antiquities of the Jews, *3.8.2)*

Phoenician coins of Tyre, minted from 126 B.C. to A.D. 65, were accepted in the temple as offerings because of their full weight of pure silver. The standard design shows a head of Melkart, and an eagle on a prow. (Actual size approximately 21 mm.)

Silver money from the Phoenician cities of Tyre, Byblos, and Sidon would have been familiar as well. Large tetradrachms, or shekels, and half shekels from Tyre were regularly used as offerings in the temple and were the only silver coins acceptable for paying the annual temple tax during the first century B.C. and later. These were readily available in the area and were of full shekel and half-shekel weight. The fact that they featured an image of the Phoenician god Melkart must have been seen as secondary to the need for a coin that was made of good silver and was the full weight as prescribed for the holy offering. In the Talmud, Tosephta Kethuboth 13, 20 states: "Silver, whenever mentioned in the Pentateuch, is Tyrian silver." The Tyrian shekel is referred to by name at one point by the historian Flavius Josephus:

> *He then bought up all the oil, paying Tyrian coin of the value of four Athenian drachms for four amphorae and proceeded to sell half an amphora at the same price.* (The Jewish War, *2.21.2, 592)*

The coins of Sidon were probably used for many years in large commercial transactions. These coins were produced in one and two-shekel sizes, as well as a number of smaller fractions, much like the coins of Tyre. Some attractive two-shekel coins of Sidon that were made in mid-fourth century B.C. depict the figure of a Persian king in a horse-drawn chariot, followed by an Egyptian attendant. Other similar pieces show the same scene with a different type of attendant.

Both seem to be propaganda pieces attesting to some now forgotten fortunes of war.

The coins of Sidon must have been familiar to the Jews in the mid-fourth century B.C. for their use as international trade silver. This large double-shekel piece shows the Persian king in a chariot with an Egyptian attendant. (Actual size approximately 30 mm.)

Some of the double-shekel coins from Sidon show the king of Persia in a chariot with a Phoenician attendant. These large coins could only be used for major purchases, as they represented more than a week's pay for most workers. (Actual size approximately 26 mm.)

The first true Jewish coins were struck between about 375 and 333 B.C. It cannot be determined if they were authorized by the Jewish high priest or some local Persian governor. The coins were crudely made, tiny silver pieces with the Hebrew inscription "Yehud," the Aramaic name for Judaea. Some of the pieces imitated the coins of Egypt or Athens with an owl on the reverse; others made use of a lily and eagle. These coins—rare today—must have been very limited in the quantities struck, and possibly intended to be more symbolic than for the convenience of trade.

Facts & Folklore

Pamphylia, Aspendos, c. 330–250 B.C. A silver stater. On the reverse is a slinger in the classic throwing stance. Many of the lead sling shot, called ballistae, have Greek inscriptions.

As a youngster, I was fascinated by biblical stories of King David, and especially the account of how, when he was young, he fought and slew the giant Goliath. The famous story is in the First Book of Samuel 17:34–36. It was likely written in the seventh or sixth century B.C., but it contains certain anachronisms largely due to the way it has been interpreted.

Ballistae used by soldiers, and perhaps by David against Goliath.

In essence, the Philistine Goliath was a gigantic, experienced warrior whom no Israelite dared to resist, and David was a mere shepherd boy who volunteered to fight on behalf of the Israelites, using only a sling, five smooth rocks, and his staff. David killed the champion with a well-placed shot to his head and would go on to become king of Israel.

The sling he used was a ubiquitous weapon consisting of a simple leather strap used to propel a stone or weighted object. Its use is shown on a contemporary silver coin of Pamphylia. In military use, the slingers often used almond-shaped lead *ballistae* (ballistic missiles) with inscribed legends insulting their opponents.

David and Goliath, Guillaume Courtois (c. 1650–1660).

From about 375 to 333 B.C., tiny silver coins were made by some Jewish authority. They imitate coins of other nations but are crudely made and often show designs on only one side. The inscription "Yehud," the Aramaic name for Judaea, is found on some of them. (Actual size approximately 10 mm.)

Judaea remained a province of the Persian Empire until 332 B.C., when Alexander the Great made himself master of the area, as he moved to conquer what was nearly the entire known world at that time. His amazing conquests and vast empire profoundly influenced the region through the spread of Greek culture, language, and, of course, the coins that he issued to accommodate trade and commerce.

***Alexander the Great in the Temple of Jerusalem*, Sebastiano Conca (c. 1736).**

The coinage of Alexander the Great of Macedonia was in use throughout his vast kingdom, which included the Holy Land that he liberated from the Persian Empire in 333 B.C. His silver tetradrachms were the same weight as a shekel. (Actual size approximately 27 mm.)

Alexander III (the Great) of Macedon ruled from 336 to 323 B.C. Under his governance, the Jews were treated well and prospered. He founded a Jewish colony in Alexandria, Egypt, and it is from scholars in that settlement that we have received the original Greek translation of the Old Testament known as the Septuagint, or "Version of the Seventy." The cordial relations that existed between Alexander and the Jews can be traced to a friendly visit he paid to Jerusalem. There he was met by Juddua the High Priest, who read to him from the Book of Daniel where it states that a Greek would destroy the Persians (Daniel 7:6; 11:3; 8:3, 20–22). Alexander rejoiced in applying this prophecy to himself, causing him to look favorably on the Jews and their religion.

After the conquest of Persia, great quantities of its gold darics and silver sigloi were melted by Alexander and used to make his own coins. This was the custom in the various countries he subjugated and the reason for his extensive coinage bearing the head of Hercules (some say it is Alexander's portrait) on one side, and the seated figure of Zeus on the other. The gold staters that Alexander and his half-brother Philip issued had a helmeted head of Pallas Athena on the obverse and a winged figure known as Nike on the reverse. Some of these coins were struck in Palestine, Joppa, and Scythopolis in Samaria. All are biblical place-names, and evidence of the extensive use of Alexandrian coinage by the Jews, despite the inclusion of graven images that must have seemed offensive to them.

Gold staters of Macedon were used in trade throughout the ancient world and were likely an acceptable form of money for any large transactions mentioned in the Bible. (Actual size approximately 18 mm.)

In time it became necessary, and customary, for the people of Judaea to use coins of Alexander and his successors, as well as other similar coins, as a common monetary unit. The transition was an easy one because the standard coinage of Alexander was based on a silver drachma equivalent to one-quarter shekel. His tetradrachm, the most common trade coin of the day, was a four-drachma silver piece that equaled one shekel in weight.

Alexander died in 323 at the age of 33, while he was still a young and successful leader. The Jews had cause to mourn his passing, which placed them under new subjugation as his empire entered a state of civil war among his ambitious generals, or successors, who fought over and divided the kingdom among themselves. The people of the Holy Land were soon pushed back and forth between two of Alexander's generals. They came under the rule of the Ptolemies of Egypt during the third century B.C., and later became subjected to the Seleucid kings of Syria.

Seleucus I, a Macedonian, had been one of Alexander's very close companions, and because of his great military skills he was given several minor command posts. After Alexander's death, he played a leading part in the ensuing division of the empire. In 321 B.C. he was rewarded with the governorship of the Satrapy of Babylon. At first, he coined money with the name and type of Alexander the Great, but in 305 he followed the examples set by his equals and assumed the title of king, which he used on his coins thereafter.

Ptolemy I of Egypt gained control of the Holy Land after the death of Alexander in 323 B.C. He issued silver tetradrachms with his portrait on one side and an eagle on the other. (Actual size approximately 27 mm.)

Babylonian silver tetradrachm of Seleucus I, 312–281 B.C.

During a rivalry between the Egyptian and Syrian kings, the territory of Palestine passed to Antiochus III of Syria, whose portrait is shown on his silver tetradrachms.

Ptolemy V of Egypt, who was unsuccessful in his efforts to retain control of Palestine and the Holy Land, was defeated in 198 B.C. by Antiochus. (Actual size approximately 28 mm.)

With Syria under the Seleucids to the north, and Egypt, ruled by the Ptolemies, to the south, Palestine was in the midst of constant bickering and warfare. In 198 B.C. the Syrians under Antiochus III defeated Scopas, the general of Ptolemy V, at Panium in North Palestine, and Judaea passed definitely to the Syrians. Flush with success, Antiochus swept through Asia Minor, seizing cities and provinces that had once been under Seleucid rule. Rhodes, Pergamum, and many of the captured cities appealed to Rome, which responded in 191 B.C. by utterly routing Antiochus and his Syrian army at the great battle of Magnesia.

Throughout this turmoil, Palestine remained under Syrian control and even prospered under the relaxed edicts of Antiochus III, who rescinded the taxes on Jerusalemites and even contributed to the temple. He also granted Jews the right to live according "to their ancestral laws." That partial autonomy changed abruptly when Antiochus IV came to power in 175 B.C., and the Jews began to learn the meaning of his wrath. Antiochus appears to have vented his vexation upon the Jews by adopting a policy of breaking the power of their priesthood, despoiling their temple, and substituting the worship of Zeus for that of Jehovah.

A silver tetradrachm of Antiochus IV, the Greek king of Syria, 175–164 B.C. Antiochus looted the temple treasury, destroyed holy texts, and defiled the altar by sacrificing a pig, in an effort to Hellenize the Jews. He only succeeded in igniting the Maccabean Revolt, which ultimately granted a degree of temporary freedom for the Jews. (Actual size approximately 33 mm.)

Antiochus IV intended to foster Greek culture and religion among his subjects through this suppression, but the results were quite the opposite. His coins use the title "Epiphanes" or "God Made Manifest," but his contemporaries referred to him as Antiochus Epimanes, "the mad." Among his many insults to the Jews, he burned the Torah and defiled the temple by sacrificing a sow upon the altar, in an effort to make the Jews conform to the Greek way of life.

> *The wicked Jason sent from Jerusalem sinful men to carry three hundred didrachmas of silver for the sacrifice of Hercules. (2 Maccabees 4:19)*

The offenses to the Jews continued through 167 B.C. when King Antiochus looted the temple, killed thousands of Jews, and sold thousands more into slavery. Many of the citizens of Jerusalem fled in fear; others, refusing to abandon their faith, went into hiding. It was at this time that Judas, the son of a priest called Mattathias, led a revolt against the king, who was soundly defeated in 164 B.C. by Judas and his brothers, known as the "Maccabees."

The Maccabees receive their father's blessing.

There is little good that can be said of King Antiochus IV except that were it not for the stunning victory of the Jewish resistance fighters, Judaism as it is known today might be very different. After the Maccabees recaptured Jerusalem from the Syrians and cleansed and rededicated the holy temple, it was a time for celebration. The original festival must have involved distributing the spoils of war, including coins of Antiochus. The largest of them were the silver tetradrachms, or shekels, with the portrait of the king on one side and the seated figure of Zeus on the other. Minor copper coins may have been given to children. The event is still remembered today in the custom of giving gifts of coins, called *Hanukah gelt*, each year during the feast of Hanukah.

COINS OF THE MACCABEES

In the relatively peaceful century following the rebellion, the Jews were granted the authority to mint coins of their own under the rule of the Hasmonean dynasty. Under the reign of Syrian King Antiochus VII, a decree was issued to Simon the High Priest that has been recorded in the First Book of Maccabees 15:6–7 as follows:

> *And I give thee leave to coin thy own money in thy country. And let Jerusalem be holy and free, and all the armor that hath been made, and the fortresses which thou hast built, and which thou keep in thy hands, let them remain to thee.*

The first coins struck under this edict were small bronze pieces issued in Jerusalem by John Hyrcanus I, as a vassal of Antiochus VII, around 132–130 B.C. John was the son of Simon the Maccabee, and the nephew of the revolutionary hero Judas Maccabee. On the obverse of these bronze coins is a lily, an often-used flower decoration for the temple and priestly robes. The reverse shows an upside-down anchor, as it would be stored on a galley ready for use. The name of Antiochus is written in Greek on either side of the anchor. The persistent use of the anchor during the next 100 years of coinage referenced the earlier Seleucid coinage and referred to the importance of the seacoast cities of the Holy Land.

A turning point in Jewish independence came when Syrian King Antiochus VII granted permission for the Jews to coin money in their own name. Silver tetradrachms of Antiochus show the king's portrait on coins he minted from 138 to 129 B.C. (Actual size approximately 30 mm.)

The first coins minted for Jerusalem were small Syrian coppers with a lily on one side and an anchor on the reverse. (Actual size approximately 14 mm.)

A bronze prutah of John Hyrcanus I, 130–104 B.C., with an inscription indicating he was high priest and head of the council of the Jews. Hyrcanus built a sound foundation for the new Judaean kingdom. (Actual size approximately 14 mm.)

John Hyrcanus I, as high priest, continued this extensive minting from 130 to 104 B.C. These were small bronze pieces known as *prutot* and *lepta* that most often featured a double cornucopia adorned with ribbons, and a pomegranate or poppy in the middle. On the other side is the Paleo-Hebrew inscription "Yehohana the High Priest and the Council of the Jews," surrounded by a wreath.

The prutah (plural, prutot) was a small bronze coin hardly any larger than a small fingernail. The lepton (plural, lepta) was equal to one-half prutah. Lepta were usually about the same diameter as prutot, but thinner and about half the weight. During the Hasmonean (or Maccabean) period, the Greek silver drachma seems to have been valued at 336 lepta or 168 prutot. The shekel was valued at 384 prutot. The Roman denarius was estimated to be worth 96 prutot. Their exchange rate, however, varied somewhat according to their size, state of preservation, type of transaction, and a moneychanger's commission, if that was included.

Judah Aristobulus I (104–103 B.C.) was the oldest son of Hyrcanus and, according to Josephus, is the first Hasmonean to use the title "king," though none of his coins expresses that. His coins were nearly identical to those of his father, with a double cornucopia on the obverse and a Hebrew inscription on the reverse.

Bronze prutot and lepta of Alexander Jannaeus, the younger brother of Judah Aristobulus I, were issued from 104 to 76 B.C. On the obverse of the most common types is an anchor with "King Alexander" in Greek. The reverse has a star of eight rays and sometimes has Hebrew letters between the rays or around the outside. A much scarcer coin of his displays an anchor and lily. The famous "widow's mite" described in the New Testament parable could have been any small bronze coin, but it most likely was one of Alexander Jannaeus because his coins were so prevalent at the time.

The small, crude anchor/star coins were likely minted after Jannaeus's death as well, during the years when John Hyrcanus II (76 to 40 B.C.) was engaged in a civil war with his brother Aristobulus II and sought the aid of Pompey the Great of Rome. Then Pompey besieged Jerusalem, defeated Aristobulus, and installed John as the "ethnarch," or ruler of the people.

The power behind the throne during the reign of Hyrcanus II had been Antipater I, the father of Herod I, who founded the Herodian dynasty. When Antipater was made procurator, Herod, though only 25, obtained the government of Galilee. After the death of Julius Caesar in 44 B.C., Herod at first supported Cassius, but after Mark Antony went to Syria in 41 B.C. and sought his favor, Herod was eventually made king of Judaea.

Mattathias Antigonus, the last Hasmonean king, initiated several changes in the coins that he issued during his short reign from 40 to 37 B.C. His Hebrew name is shown on his prutah coins, and the pomegranate between the double cornucopia is replaced by an ear of barley. His name is also on the two larger denominations he issued, which can be compared in value with the Seleucid chalcous and dichalcous. He was also the only Jewish ruler to depict the holy vessels of the Temple of Jerusalem on his coins. Mattathias was the son of Aristobulus II. He attempted to rule with the aid of the Parthian King Orodes II, allegedly through gifts that included 500 Jewish women. Mattathias, with help from the Parthian army, occupied Jerusalem and laid claim to the office of High Priest. Herod I (called the Great), who was governor of Galilee at the time, fled to Rome to enlist support and was officially designated king of Judaea. Herod and the

Roman legions besieged Jerusalem and captured it in 37 B.C. The ensuing execution of Mattathias brought an end to the Hasmonean dynasty.

Judah Aristobulus I proclaimed himself king, but he remained in power only from 104–103 B.C. He was the eldest son of Hyrcanus I and issued bronze prutot of the same design as his father. (Actual size approximately 14 mm.)

Several different types of small bronze coins were made by Alexander Jannaeus, 103–76 B.C. The most common of these has a star of eight rays, sometimes with letters between the rays or near the rim. The obverse shows an inverted anchor. His bronze lepta are most likely the tiny "widow's mite" of New Testament fame. (Actual size approximately 15 mm.)

Bronze prutot, or two-lepta coins, were minted for John Hyrcanus II, who ruled in 67 B.C. and again from 63 to 40. He was engaged in a civil war with his brother Aristobulus II during much of that time, before he was installed by Pompey the Great as "ruler of the people." (Actual size approximately 14 mm.)

Mattathias Antigonus initiated several changes in the coins he issued from 40 to 37 B.C. On some of his bronze prutot, an ear of barley replaces the pomegranate between the double cornucopia. (Actual size approximately 14 mm.)

THE ROMAN INFLUENCE

In the first century B.C. the Greek empire gradually fell to the Romans, who took Corinth in 146 B.C. and Athens in 86 B.C., after the city-state revolted. Julius Caesar conquered Gaul and Pompey brought Syria and Palestine under Roman control, then occupied Jerusalem in 63 B.C. Both Aristobulus and Hyrcanus appealed to Pompey for support of their leadership claims; Pompey was quick to enter into Jewish politics and decided in favor of Hyrcanus. At that point, warfare broke out anew between followers of the brothers, ending when Aristobulus and his two sons were carried off to Rome and paraded through the streets in disgrace.

A Roman denarius of M. Aemilius Scaurus, who was sent by Pompey in 64 B.C. to settle the dispute between the warring Maccabee brothers. The surrender in 62 B.C. of Aretas III, the Nabataean king, was commemorated by this coin issued in 58 B.C. (Actual size approximately 18 mm.)

In 58 B.C. a special Roman silver denarius was struck to commemorate the defeat, by Pompey's general Marcus Scaurus, of the Nabataean King Aretas III, who supported Hyrcanus II in his battles against Aristobulus. The design shows Aretas kneeling in an attitude of submission. A similar Roman commemorative coin was issued in 54 B.C. to proclaim the capture of Aristobulus and his submission to Rome. The design on that coin shows a bearded Jew kneeling beside a camel, yielding to Rome by extending a symbolic palm branch.

This Roman denarius was minted by Aulus Plautius in 54 B.C. to commemorate the defeat of King Aretas. The inscription "Bacchius Judaeus" refers to Aristobulus, who made his submission to Pompey. (Actual size approximately 18 mm.)

After Syria became a Roman province, Pompey appointed Aulus Gabinius as proconsul of Judaea, and in 57 B.C. Gabinius then reinstalled Hyrcanus as high priest of Jerusalem. He also worked to suppress the revolts and introduced important changes in the government of Judaea. One of Gabinius's reforms was the issuance of silver tetradrachms made in imitation of the familiar coins of the former king of Syria, Philip Philadelphus. The new coins were issued for a period of about 30 years and can be distinguished only by special dates and symbols.

Tetradrachm of Philip Philadelphus (94–83 B.C.). (Actual size 27 mm.)

Silver tetradrachms imitating those of Syrian King Philip Philadelphus were issued during the Roman occupation of Jerusalem. The coins of Aulus Gabinius, 57–55 B.C., and his successors can be distinguished by a monogram near the leg of Zeus on the reverse, and distinctive dates below the design. (Actual size approximately 26 mm.)

The original coins of Philip Philadelphus, who ruled from 94 to 83 B.C., were more carefully fashioned yet similar in appearance to those made during the Roman occupation. His epithet "Brother Lover" likely referred to Antiochus XI, who shared the throne with him and is thought to have been his twin. Philip's rule lasted only until the Armenian King Tigranes II conquered Syria in 83 B.C.

A tetradrachm of Armenian King Tigranes II.

The Romans brought law, order, and stability to the nations they ruled, but that peace was maintained by garrisons of soldiers, whose presence was not generally appreciated. Foreign legions were stationed in Palestine, and there were heavy taxes to pay. The atmosphere was highly charged and revolt, especially where the Jewish religion was concerned, was a constant danger. In 31 B.C. Octavian, later known as Caesar Augustus, became the first ruler of the Roman Empire. It was during his reign that Jesus was born.

Chapter 4

Coins in the New Testament

The final Old Testament–era issue of tiny Jewish bronze prutah coins was made by Herod the Great, who ruled from 40 to 4 B.C. They can be divided into two groups: those that are dated and those that are not. The dated coins all bear the same date, the year 3. This would relate to the year of his reign, equating to 37 B.C. All the legends on his coins were in Greek, and no Hebrew legends appear on any coins of the Herodian dynasty. The values of his coins were 8, 4, and 2 prutot, and a number of smaller bronze lepta.

Herod I, the Great, was governor of Galilee from 40 to 4 B.C. A man without mercy, he had two of his sons and his wife executed and later ordered the mass murder of all Jewish male infants anywhere near Bethlehem, where he heard a future king of the Jews would be born. He issued many different bronze coins. The largest was an eight-prutot coin showing a helmet on the obverse and a tripod and bowl on the reverse. (Actual size approximately 22 mm.)

A bronze two-prutot coin of Herod I, the Great, showing a tripod table flanked by palm branches. (Actual size approximately 18 mm.)

A bronze prutah of Herod I with his inscription on the obverse and an anchor on the reverse. (Actual size approximately 13 mm.)

Emblems on Herod's coins included a tripod, prow, caduceus, pomegranate, shield, helmet, palm branch, eagle, anchor, and cornucopia. The wide selection of types without graven images was an indication that Herod did not want to offend the religious feelings of his subjects. The inscriptions show his name and title in Greek only.

Herod was not known as "the Great" during his lifetime—he was a tyrannical man, feared and respected by men and nations. Typical of his atrocious cruelties was the murder of all but two members of the Supreme Council when he became king. He was known for a love of Greek culture, but also for a tendency toward violent jealousies and passions, leading to the murder of his wife Mariamne and his sons Alexander and Aristobulus. He married ten wives in all.

Among Herod's undertakings were the restoration of the Temple of Jerusalem and the city of Samaria, which he called Sebaste. Some believe that the temple was built to satisfy his artistic taste rather than his religious instincts. He expanded a small town on the seacoast to a great city known as Caesarea and is credited with introducing Greek games to his subjects. He was also very much involved in the biblical account of the Nativity.

***The Magi in the House of Herod*, James Tissot (c. 1886–1894).**

> *And when he had gathered all the chief priests and scribes of the people together, he demanded of them where Christ should be born. And they said unto him, "In Bethlehem of Judaea for thus it is written by the prophet." . . . Then Herod called the wise men, inquired of them diligently what time the star appeared. And he sent them to Bethlehem, and said, "Go and search diligently for the young child; and when you have found*

him, bring me word again that I may come and worship him also." . . . The wise men followed the star and reached the manger. They fell down and worshipped him, and when they opened their treasures, they presented unto him gifts; gold, frankincense and myrrh. . . . And when they were departed, behold the angel of the Lord appeared to Joseph in a dream saying, "Arise, and take the young child and his mother, and flee into Egypt . . . for Herod will seek the young child to destroy him." (Matthew 2:4, 7–8, 10–11, 13)

According to the Book of Matthew, when Herod heard of the birth of an infant that some said was destined to become King of the Jews, he ordered the death of all male children up to two years of age. There are no accounts of this event in the other Gospels or contemporary historical accounts, so the details of whether and how this slaughter happened will likely remain lost to time.

[Herod] sent forth and slew all the children that were in Bethlehem and in all the coasts thereof, from two years old and under, according to the time which he had diligently inquired of the wise men. (Matthew 2:16)

It was because of this that Joseph and Mary fled to Egypt to save the life of the newborn Jesus. They remained there until Herod died, before returning to the land of Israel.

But when they heard that Archelaus did reign in Judaea . . . he turned aside into the parts of Galilee; and he came and dwelt in a city called Nazareth. (Matthew 2:22–23)

These accounts of the birth and early childhood of Jesus are at odds with the chronology of that time. It is clear that Herod died in 4 B.C., and thus the Nativity must have occurred prior to that. Exactly when remains a mystery, but the best assumptions place the event between what we commonly consider 7 and 4 B.C.

COINS OF THE YEAR THAT JESUS WAS BORN

There are no coins known today that can be traced to the year zero—indeed, that year does not exist. The Gregorian calendar, as we know it today, turned from December 31, 1 B.C. to January 1, A.D. 1—those dates having been arbitrarily assigned to correspond with what was once widely believed to have been the birth year of Jesus. The general use of such dating was not employed until sometime around the sixth century, and no year zero was assigned to the timeline. The customary use of Christian dating on coins did not begin until 1234, and then it was used only very occasionally until around the year 1500.

What, then, was being used for money at the time and place of the birth of Jesus? To answer that, we must consider what was available in the district around Judaea in the period close to 6/5 B.C. Coins at that time were usually traded by weight, with little regard for when or where they were made. Thus, it would not have been uncommon for any coin from neighboring districts to be passed in circulation, from the old Hasmonean coppers to the more recent Herodian coppers. Larger Roman copper, bronze, and silver coins would have been used in commerce and to pay necessary taxes. None of those coins, however, was ever dated in a way that was specific to the year of the Holy Birth.

One of the coins that can be dated close to the beginning of the Christian era is a silver tetradrachm of Antioch in the region of Seleucia and Pieria. It was struck in year 31 of the Actian Era and corresponds to 1 B.C./A.D. 1. The date consists of Greek letters with the numeric values of 1 plus 30, in that order. Greek cities that used the Actian Era started their calendar on September 12, 31 B.C., the date when Octavianus (Octavian) defeated Mark Antony in the sea battle at Actium in northwestern Greece. The coin struck 31 years later was made on the eve of what we now calculate as the beginning of A.D. 1.

An Antioch silver tetradrachm of Augustus dated year 28, which equates to 4/3 B.C. (Actual size approximately 26 mm.)

A bronze coin of Augustus made in 5/4 B.C. in Antioch, near the time of Jesus's birth. (Actual size approximately 23 mm.)

Tetradrachms of this same design were issued in other years besides the year 27 and would relate to the Christian calendar year of 5/4 B.C. The split-year reckoning is a result of their year beginning and ending on months that were other than January and December as in the modern cycle. Those coins were minted about 400 miles away from Bethlehem, but they are the closest known to the time and place where Jesus was born.

A second, somewhat similar coin, also made in that same district of Seleucia and Pieria under the emperorship of Augustus, is a copper piece about 23 mm in diameter. The inscription on this coin also dates it to the year 27 of the Actian calendar, or precisely 5/4 B.C., which could have been the very year of the Nativity.

The large silver shekels of Tyre, commonly used as temple offerings, were also dated with years that can be translated to correspond with modern Christian reckoning. All of the Tyrian coins have dates that begin in 126/125 B.C. and continue almost uninterrupted until the time of the first Jewish revolt against Rome, in A.D. 66–70. Curiously, only a few of them are specifically dated to the decades just before or after the beginning of the Christian era. Those that were made after 17 B.C. are believed to have been minted in Jerusalem rather than Tyre.

ENROLLMENT AND THE STAR OF BETHLEHEM

> *And it came to pass that in those days there went out a decree from Caesar Augustus, that the whole world should be enrolled. This enrolling was first made by Cyrenius (Quirinius), the governor of Syria. And all went to be enrolled, every one into his own city, and Joseph also went up from Galilee, out of the city of Nazareth into Judea, to the city of David, which is called Bethlehem; because he was of the house and family of David, to be enrolled with Mary his espoused wife, who was with child. (Luke 2:1–5)*

The census, or enrollment, that was ordered by the Roman Emperor Augustus was for the purpose of taxation throughout the kingdom. This was the event that caused Joseph and Mary to go to Bethlehem. It is likely that the half-shekel tax would have been a Tyrian coin, or two silver denarii, which were the equivalent in Roman money. Any of the silver pieces made by Augustus after he became emperor in 27 B.C. would have been likely candidates for use.

The census ordered by Roman Emperor Augustus was for the purpose of taxation. Joseph would have paid two silver denarii, like this one of Augustus minted c. 15 B.C. (Actual size approximately 19 mm.)

There is no actual historical confirmation of the incident that Luke describes, and his is the only extant source of information on this subject. Yet, other known records of the existence of Quirinius as a ruler in Syria, and similar enrollments in other cities, tend to invalidate the problems raised by the conflicting account given by Jewish historian Flavius Josephus of a corresponding (second) census in A.D. 6.

The journey to Bethlehem and the birth of Jesus, as recorded in Matthew 2:1–13, were heralded by a magnificent star that led the Magi (Herod's "wise men from the East") to that site. Exactly who the Magi were, and even their exact number, is shrouded in mystery. Some accounts portray them as kings or princes; others say they were magicians or priests from the sacred cast of the Medes. If they were kings, we should be able to verify their existence through coins, but as of now that does not seem possible. There is no way to accurately trace their journey, or determine who they were or their place of origin. Equally mystifying are their gifts of gold, frankincense, and myrrh. We can only surmise that the gold would have been in the form of coins, and quite likely the still-plentiful staters of Alexander the Great.

***The Adoration of the Magi*, by Edward Burne-Jones.**

One recurring speculation tentatively identifies two of the Magi as kings, whose coins are well known to collectors today. The first of these is Gaspar, recognized as being the Indo-Greek King Gondophares, who ruled from about A.D. 19 to 46. His coins show a bearded portrait of a man who would have been much younger when he made the journey to Bethlehem.

A second identification has been suggested that links the Nabataean King Aretas and his son Malichus to the Magi. One or both of them could easily have made the 60-mile trip from the Arabian city of Nabataea to Bethlehem. Aretas IV ruled from 9 B.C. to A.D. 40. His son Malichus could well be the elusive Melchior, who legend names as one of the Magi. Copper coins of King Aretas show his portrait on one side and an inscription in Aramaic on the other.

It would have been a short journey for King Aretas IV and his son Malichus to travel from their home in Nabataea to Bethlehem. Speculation is that Malichus could have been the prince, or future king, identified in early German literature as Melchior of the Magi. The bronze prutot of Aretas, minted during his reign from 9 B.C. to A.D. 40, show the king and queen. The inscription on the reverse is in Aramaic, the language of Jesus. (Actual size approximately 20 mm.)

The Indo-Parthian King Gondophares, A.D. 20–60, may have been one of the Magi who traveled to Bethlehem. He is shown on his copper coins minted many years after the Nativity. (Actual size approximately 12 mm.)

Aramaic was the common language of the Galilean region and the language that Jesus spoke throughout his lifetime when he preached or spoke to friends. He would have used Hebrew in conversations

Facts & Folklore

Did this unusual coin refer to the Star of Bethlehem?

This copper coin of Syria, Seleucia and Pieria was minted under Emperor Augustus and dated Year 43 of the Actian Era, which equals A.D. 12 in the Christian calendar.

The unusual design on this coin might well have been based on the Star of Bethlehem, and was minted about 15 years after the celestial event. The Ram is the Aries zodiac symbol for the stellar constellation referred to by star-gazers and the Magi. The astrological symbol of the Ram goes back to Babylonian times, when it was associated with agriculture and the god of shepherds. Regarding the precise date of the appearance of the star, many astronomers agree that it was an actual occurrence, though its exact nature is unknown, and likely happened sometime around 4–3 B.C. One factor in establishing the date is that Joseph went to Bethlehem to pay his tax, and that would have occurred at a very specific time.

A constellation map by Johann Bayer from 1603, including the astrological symbol Aries.

with religious leaders and when reading in the synagogue. His name in the Aramaic language was *Yeshua bar Yosef* (Jesus son of Joseph).

That the Magi believed a star led them on their journey is clear from the words used in Matthew 2:2. Astronomers have proposed that it was not a star, but a comet. Others say it was a conjunction of the planets Jupiter and Saturn (7 B.C.), or Jupiter and Venus (6 B.C.); another theory is that it may have been a stella nova, a star that suddenly increases in magnitude and brilliance and then fades away. The event, whatever it may have been, was never recorded on any coin with certainty, though it was not unusual to include stars or comets in coin designs at that time.

City street in the remains of Gerash (ancient Gerasa) in Jordan.

Chapter 5

Life in the New Testament

Have you ever used a dial telephone, a slide rule, or an ink-loaded fountain pen? Probably not if you were born in the twenty-first century. You might even have to Google those words to understand what those things were, or how they were used in everyday life not long before you were born. And only shortly before that, your parents and grandparents had to communicate by writing and mailing letters, do simple arithmetic without a calculator, and somehow get by without television or the internet.

We live in a constantly changing world where customs, ideas, and advancements in technology are ever fluid. Fortunately, this has been the overall trend for millennia. New innovations bring about changes that are soon adopted by the masses, and the old ways fade away and are soon forgotten. Imagine then, how different life must have been two or three thousand years ago. And sometimes, with few written records of events covering everyday life, we can only wonder what life was like for the common man in those distant, ancient settings.

The most accurate and detailed accounts of ancient life are found in the Bible and other contemporary writings, memorials, and structures that have survived the tests of time. My personal interest, as stated previously, is in learning about contemporary events through their use of coins and money. Beyond that, there is a plethora of published studies available to all through books and online resources.

Most people who lived in and around Judaea in the first century were not much different than most of us today. Of course, they did not have any of the modern conveniences we enjoy, but they worked, played, dined, paid taxes, married, and raised families. Life for Jesus at that time was very much the same as others of that era, and undoubtedly, he led a rather normal life prior to his ministry while he "increased in wisdom and stature, and favor with God and man" (Luke 2:52).

Through the gospels, we learn that Jesus began his mission after His baptism by John, near the river Jordan, and ended at the time of the Last Supper with his disciples. Luke 3:23 states the Jesus was "about 30 years of age" at that time. There are numerous accounts of the nativity in Bethlehem, with a few glimpses of Jesus's early childhood, but we have only scattered information about his education in the temple and his likely apprenticeship in his father's carpentry shop. Many men at that time simply farmed to feed and support their families, while others were businessmen, merchants, builders, teachers, bakers, and physicians.

A typical first-century Jewish family might begin with a man in his 20s, his teenaged wife, and, in time, two or three children. In those days, marriage took place in two stages. The formal betrothal would first be agreed upon between the husband and the girl's father. Several months to a year later, the girl would move into her new husband's house. It wasn't until they began living together that the marriage became official.

Life at the time revolved mainly around the synagogue, tradition, and hard labor to feed and provide for their needs. Their greatest adversity was being subjected to the strict, punitive domination and taxation by occupying forces such as the Greeks or Romans. The message preached by Jesus was for people to live by faith in God's provision, and not to be obsessed with worldly goods.

Existing archaeological and numismatic evidence provide detailed views of many of the places, customs, and items in daily use during those times. Some of these are not vastly different than their counterparts today. Finger rings and earrings were as popular then as now. Books (scrolls) and writing instruments were used by educated scholars; some tools, medical equipment, and weapons are easily recognizable for what they are, though not nearly as sophisticated as today's equivalents. Pottery, oil lamps, and tableware would be familiar to all. Their ancient bread, beer, and wine would still appeal to modern tastes. The need and use of money for trade, barter, and taxes is still universal. Examples of many of these items can be seen throughout this book, as well as in museums and online.

The personal possessions and minute objects of ordinary citizens are frequently some of the most illuminating artifacts studied by archeologists. This includes their coins, religious icons, pottery, lamps, and weapons. In the case of the ancient Israelites, however, the availability of these artifacts has been influenced by religious customs and principles, the most rigorous of which is found in the Book of Deuteronomy, where God charged the people of Israel with the commandment, "Thou shalt not make unto thee any graven image."

The iconoclastic nature of those words, written on stone tablets by the finger of God, were a stern warning against making or using images of any nature. Although no single biblical passage contains a full definition of idolatry, the meaning is clear that the adoration of idols or images was to be strictly forbidden, as was the worship of any polytheistic gods.

In adherence to the sacred word, most Holy Land objects are devoid of images or references to deities, instead displaying objects of natural beauty and design. In most cases, utilitarian objects are modest in form and undecorated. Objects found at Qumran included small, simple jugs, flasks, drinking cups, pots, dishes, oil lamps, and shards used for writing notes.

Personal hygiene was another essential element. Bathing usually involved the use of cleansing oils; cosmetics were essential for women, and hair styling and trimming were customary, as was concern for a man's beard. Adult men wore full facial hair, and it is believed that Jesus followed that tradition. This was a style quite different from the clean-shaven look devised by Alexander the Great as a defense for his soldiers, to prevent their beards from being held by an opponent in battle.

POTTERY

To archeologists, finds of pottery offer vital information about the location, age, and culture of the users. That basic material was universally useful because it is readily available, easy to shape and work with, and can be made waterproof. It is estimated that clay pottery was first made in China thousands of years ago, by making a long coil of clay and shaping it into a pot or cup, then heating it in an oven. As methods and needs grew, people began to use artistic designs to show their individual and cultural identities.

The use of clay pottery by ancient Israelites dates back to a time when Phoenician potters sold or traded their products throughout the region. An early reference to this is found in 2 Samuel 17:28: "When David came to Mahanaim . . . They brought beds, basins and earthen vessels." Even earlier than that, the use of simple clay pottery seems to have begun in the Neolithic era, reaching Palestine and surrounding areas between 7000 and 6000 B.C.

Earthenware pottery was made from clay that was turned on a spinning disc and molded by hand into the desired shape. Simple items could be hand-formed, while more delicate or decorated items were artfully sculped and painted before being fired, glazed, or hardened. The firing process makes pottery sturdy and long-lasting, part of the reason why many have survived across centuries to be found by archaeologists. Finely made pieces were sometimes stamped with the potter's seal or a special foundry mark.

The Etruscans, who ruled most of Italy in the sixth and fifth centuries B.C., are known to have made two types of pottery: fancy, expensive pieces and plain, inexpensive items for everyday use. They began by making black-figure pottery, later followed the Greeks by making red-figure pottery.

A red-figure Greek *skyphos* cup, c. 350 B.C.

Although Roman pottery began with Etruscan-style designs, it soon developed a tradition of its own. Potters in Italy tended to make their pots in only one color. They didn't paint pictures on them the way potters did in Greece, instead using molds to create decorations by shaping the clay. That was much faster and cheaper than painting, so those factories could make great quality pottery and sell it very cheaply, thus extending their sales to many nearby regions.

The pottery produced in Rome was mostly for utilitarian purposes. It is found all over the former Roman Empire and beyond. One of the most popular items was the classic amphora, a large two-handled vessel used for transporting and storing liquids such as wines and the Spanish olive oil that was widely used for lighting, cooking, and washing. Other specialty items included dolls, spindle whorls, identity stamps, toilet seats, water pipes, and even ovens.

Clay pottery vessels are generally classified as four major Greek styles: geometric, Corinthian, black-figure, and red-figure.

Storage and transport vessels included jars of various shapes like the *amphora*, *pithos*, *pelike*, *hydria*, *stamnos*, and *pyxis*.

Mixing vessels, especially that for the symposia (an all-male drinking party), were the *krater* and *kyathos*.

Jugs and cups, as well as several types of *kylix*, included *kantharos*, *phiale*, *skyphos*, *mastos*, or *rhyton*. Others included *oinochoe* and *loutrophoros*.

Vases for oils, perfumes, and cosmetics included the large *lekythos* and the smaller *aryballos*, *alabastron*, and *askos*.

A Greek kantharos with black-figure designs of a bull and lions, from the sixth century B.C

A Roman hydria bowl from the first century A.D.

A rather humorous design on a fifth-century B.C. Macedonian silver tetradrachm of Mende, depicting the inebriated Dionysus riding on the back of an ass, still holding his *kantharos*, as he is being carried home from a symposium. This was an event that linked the world of men with the Olympian gods—at least until the morning!

A more utilitarian use of pottery can be seen on a fourth-century B.C. bronze coin of Krannon in Thessaly. This coin displays a *hydria* being transported on a wagon, perhaps to quench a fire, or to deliver wines or oil.

BOWLS, CUPS, BLADES, AND PLATES

Common first-century tableware.

It is easy to envision a normal family meal, eaten at table with things that would be familiar today. Most of the items would have been simple earthenware bowls, serving plates, tableware, cups, and dishes.

I have previously commented on the drinking cup, or "Holy Grail," in the introduction on page xvi. Illustrated below is a typical example of the type of goblet, or drinking cup, that was likely used at the Last Supper, as well as some vials.

> *And as they were eating, he took bread, and after blessing it broke it and gave it to them, said, "Take; this is my body." And he took a cup, and when he had given thanks, he gave it to them, and they all drank of it.* (Mark 14:22–25)

The phrase "holy grail" is never mentioned in any Bible passages, and the meaning, while unclear, seems to have originated with subsequent legends and devotion to the seminal supper. Others consider it to be a vessel used by Joseph of Arimathea to collect the blood of Jesus after the crucifixion. In that case, the container would most likely have been what is commonly known as a "tear vial," a small glass bottle that was used by mourners to preserve their tears at the death of a loved one.

The Holy Grail? A typical first-century wine cup.

If anything other than ordinary drinking cups had been owned by the apostles, they likely would have been sold, and the money given to the poor and needy.

> *For the poor shall never cease out of the land: therefore I command thee, saying, "Thou shalt open thine hand wide unto thy brother, to thy poor, and to thy needy, in thy land." (Deuteronomy 15:11)*

LAMPS AND OTHER HOUSEHOLD ITEMS

Wood has long been a convenient medium for making useful items of all sorts, from cups and bowls to clubs, boxes, tools, combs, dreidels, and ladles. Unfortunately, such items are rarely seen from the late Roman period in the Near East. The unusually arid climate at Qumran, however, preserved many archeological finds to grant us a vivid view of life during biblical times and ancient woodworking techniques we might expect of the carpenter profession. Items that needed to endure, such as knives, surgical instruments, fibulae, rings, needles, nails, and weapons, were made of metal, primarily copper or brass.

(Left) A Herodian oil lamp. (Right) An oil lamp with the design of a menorah on top.

The style, importance, and use of oil lamps during that period in Judaea are also a noteworthy area of study. Of major significance is the menorah, described in the Bible as an ancient golden lampstand consisting of seven individual lamps. It was used in the tabernacle set up by Moses in the wilderness, and later in the Temple in Jerusalem. Fresh olive oil was burned daily to light its lamps. The menorah was subsequently adopted as a symbol of both Judaism and Christianity in New Testament times, though it is only considered a symbol of Judaism today.

By its very nature, light itself is a quintessential element of life and one of the first gifts from God.

> *In the beginning, God created the heaven and the earth, and the earth was without form, and void; and darkness was upon the face of the deep. And the Spirit of God moved upon the face of the waters. And God said, let there be light: and there was light. And God saw the light, that it was good. (Genesis 1:3)*

> *When Jesus spoke again to the people, he said "I am the light of the world: he that follows me shall not walk in darkness, but shall have the light of life." (John 8:12)*

It is not surprising that many prehistoric peoples believed that their only source of light, the sun, was itself a supreme deity. Sun gods have been part of the mythologies developed by cultures all over the world. Even today, the first day of the week is called Sunday, a holdover derived from the Latin *dies solis*, 'sun's day,' a pagan Roman holiday. The Judaeans, however, were more aware of the true nature of sunlight, as shown through their scripture teachings. During the time of King David, Moses, and Solomon, hand-formed clay oil lamps were well known and were referred to by David in Psalms 119:105 with an analogy to God's Word being "a lamp to my feet, and a light for my path."

The earliest Judaean oil lamps are hand-formed clay objects known as Palestinian saucer lamps. The vessels used in Old Testament times began as simple dishes or shallow pots with a palm-fiber wick, known as open saucer or pinched nozzle oil lamps.

Terracotta lamps in the Hellenistic world of Alexander the Great are identified by a longer nozzle that held the wick. By the time of Jesus, the lamp had become flatter, rounder, and with many variations and ornamentations. In Matthew 25:1–13, the story is told of the wise and foolish virgins, and their lamps:

> *At that time the kingdom of heaven will be like ten virgins who took their lamps and went out to meet the bridegroom. Five of them were foolish and five were wise. The foolish ones took their lamps but did not take any oil with them. The wise ones, however, took oil in jars along with their lamps. . . . The virgins who were ready went in with him to the wedding banquet. And the door was shut.*

In the first century B.C., Roman lamps were being mold-made with features similar to those of the Hellenistic period, but with the addition of a handle. Similar lamps used in the Holy Land are called "Hasmonean" style, after the dynasty that ruled in Judaea and the surrounding regions at that time. Discus-shaped lamps, exported from Italy, were another distinctive type of lamp from that era. These were large, concave, and often contained molded designs with elaborate scenes.

Various ancient oil lamps in bronze and clay.

Near the beginning of New Testament times, a new style of oil lamp made its appearance in Samaria. Those had vertical handles and, instead of a discus, a pronounced shoulder with decorative motifs. Early versions have a small, round body with a wide nozzle, and were often decorated with a ladder motif. Around the time of the reign of Herod the Great, another distinctive style emerged, known as Herodian lamps. These have a rounded body with a large fill-hole and splayed nozzle, and they were the most commonly used in Judaea between 25 B.C. and A.D. 150.

Metal lamps were produced in the ancient Mediterranean area, and these were also classified by types. They were popular during the Hellenistic, Roman, and Byzantine periods and are generally divided into these categories. The decorative elements of metal lamps vary greatly, especially in their lids, handles, and discus areas.

GLASS FOR THE AFFLUENT

An assortment of Roman glassware.

People of rank and wealth in biblical times could afford luxurious glass items. It is believed that the earliest glass objects were created around 3500 B.C. in Egypt.

The ancient Roman historian Pliny suggested that Phoenician merchants made the first glass, but archaeological evidence shows that the first glass vessels were more likely made in Egypt, around 1500 B.C. Around that same time, the Phoenicians invented glass-

Jewish glass vessels.

blowing, which made glass products inexpensive enough to be somewhat competitive with pottery cups, small bowls, and things like perfume containers, unguents, cosmetic bottles, and vases.

Some of the earliest evidence of glassblowing in Judaea comes from a collection of waste from a glass shop, dated from 37 to 4 B.C., including fragments of glass tubes, rods and tiny blown tear bottles, which was dumped in a mikvah, a ritual bath in the Jewish Quarter of the Old City of Jerusalem. The so-called tear vials were prevalent in ancient Roman times, when mourners filled small glass vials or cups with tears and placed them in burial tombs as symbols of love and respect for the deceased.

WORK, PROFESSIONS, AND OCCUPATIONS

Farming and other forms of food collection or production were common occupations in biblical times. How people thrived and worked to make a living mostly depended on where they lived. One such group of food providers were the fishermen mentioned in Isaiah 19:8 and Matthew 4:18. We know that many of those people were dear to Jesus, and we even know, from surviving artifacts, some of the kinds of fishhooks, lines, spears, and nets that they used.

Another common occupation, especially favored by nomadic groups, was tending to flocks of sheep and goats, and these shepherds traveled from place to place in order to feed and protect the animals that were vital to the food supply chain. More settled groups raised their crops and provided services to people in towns and urban areas. Among the most highly rated and esteemed professions were the blacksmiths, carpenters, and masons.

The Miraculous Draught of Fishes, James Tissot (c. 1886–1894).

Education was essential to the community's success, growth, and survival, and this not overlooked in the development of Hebrew culture. Here the rabbinical teachers led the way and were traditionally held in the greatest esteem for their role in preserving and sharing the accumulated knowledge, divine guidance, and ideological traditions from generation to generation.

Unfortunately, war and subjugation were also part of daily life in ancient Israel, and military service became a lifetime occupation for many. In earlier days, from the Egyptian enslavement until the time of the Persian King Darius in 486 B.C., organized resistance was scant and voluntary. Later, organized and disciplined soldiers helped bring some stability, but it was not until the First Jewish Revolt in A.D. 66 that a truly defensive conflict was waged against the Roman rulers.

Several passages in the Bible refer to both Jesus and Joseph as carpenters, and it would have been customary for a skill or profession like that to be passed on from father to son. When these references were first translated from the original Greek text, the word *téktōn* was used meaning an artisan, craftsmen, or woodworker, so describing them as carpenters is a likely way to perhaps cover multiple skills.

MONEY AND TRADE

Many different kinds of coins were used during the period from the birth of Christ to the time that biblical accounts were recorded in written form. Jesus, the apostles, and all of the participants chronicled in the Bible saw and used these coins, which we know today as ancient remainders of the past, as part of everyday life. Coins that have been passed down to us stand as testimony to the historical accuracy of the Bible.

There can be little doubt that money was important to every level of society in biblical times. It is mentioned in one of the most often repeated passages, that of 1 Timothy 6:10: "For the love of money is the root of every evil." This is also one of the most often misquoted passages, frequently rendered incorrectly as "Money is the root of all evil."

Food, a very real necessity of life, is mentioned 124 times throughout the Bible. Money, in one form or another, is mentioned 129 times, while gold (at 417) and silver (at 282) rank even higher. Sixteen of the 40 parables preached by Jesus mention coins or money, further indicating the significance of money at the time.

Numerous passages in the works of the Apostles speak about money and its role in society. Among those are Matthew 18:23–35, 20:1–16, and 25:14–30, and Luke 10:30–37, 12:16–21, 15:8–10; 16:1–13, 18:10–14, and 19:11–27. A typical example deals with interest, and the responsibility of using money wisely and dutifully.

> *And it came to pass on his arrival back again having received the kingdom, that he desired those bondmen to whom he gave the money to be called to him, in order that he might know what every one had gained by trading . . . "And did you not give my money to the bank; and I should have received it, at my coming, with interest?" (Luke 19:15, 23)*

In Old Testament times, Israelite farmers were poor and generally produced only enough for their own needs. As markets and a demand for local products grew, tradesmen became important to the

community, and merchants set up business stalls in the city. Eventually a more sophisticated international system of commerce developed, and Palestine found itself geographically well suited for both land and sea trade routes. Thus, by New Testament days there were strict regulations on foreign trade and local business.

Foreign coins flowed into the region during this time from their export of olive oil, linens, and trade goods. Coinage of Egypt, Macedonia, Phoenicia, and neighboring districts were all familiar to the Israelites because they were made on the Greek standard that closely followed the shekel in weight. Roman coins were also in daily use and were important for payments to the Roman authorities. The Roman denarius was equal in weight to one-quarter shekel of silver.

A silver drachma with the head of Hercules on the obverse and Zeus seated on the reverse, minted in the time of Philip III of Macedon, c. 325 B.C. These coins circulated widely and were the weight of one-quarter shekel. (Actual size approximately 17 mm.)

A Roman didrachma, c. 225–215, an unusual denomination that was soon replaced by the denarius. It was equal to a half-shekel. (Actual size approximately 21 mm.)

Coinage of Alexandria in Roman Egypt circulated widely throughout Palestine. This silver tetradrachm of Tiberius was minted in A.D. 21 and circulated around the same time as Jesus's life. It shows the images of both Augustus and Tiberius. (Actual size approximately 27 mm.)

In addition to international coins, the small bronze lepta and prutot that had been made by the Hasmonean and Herodian rulers were still in circulation and were in great demand for daily use. However, temple offerings could not be made in bronze, so one of the functions of the moneychangers was to convert coins to Tyrian shekels or half-shekels for use as offerings. Their fee for making the conversion was usually eight percent.

At different times during the second temple period, the Hasmonean prutot was valued anywhere from 128 to 512 prutot to a Phoenician shekel.

Working people of that time could earn approximately one denarius, or one-quarter shekel, per day for their work. That was standard pay for laborers, fishermen, and soldiers, enough to provide for the living expenses of a middle-class family. Skilled craftsmen were able to earn more, but there were very few opportunities other than for tailors, bakers, scribes, builders, and pottery makers. Joseph, who is described as being a carpenter, would have taught his son the same trade and lived a comfortable life.

> *And coming into his own country, he taught them in their synagogues, so that they wondered and said: "How came this man by this wisdom and miracles? Is not this the carpenter's son? Is not his mother called Mary?"* (Matthew 13:54–55)

Roman coins in use during the first century A.D. included gold, silver, copper, and brass pieces of several denominations, often depicting the images of the emperors who decreed their issue. These coins would have been familiar to many biblical characters and their contemporaries, and to those who later recorded the events.

Roman Emperor Nero issued this tetradrachm for use in Antioch and neighboring districts. It is dated year 10, which equates to A.D. 64, the year of the great fire that destroyed much of Rome. (Actual size approximately 25 mm.)

Throughout this time both Jews and Christians were often subjected to the wrath and cruelty of the Roman rulers, particularly as their beliefs put them in conflict with the polytheistic practices of the time. Nero was particularly harsh, and when much of Rome was destroyed during the great fire of A.D. 64, he blamed and punished the Christians for the disaster.

COST OF LIVING

Raising a family was as challenging in biblical times as it is today. Providing for food and shelter, paying taxes, and seeing that sons

Jesus turns water into wine at the wedding in Cana.

were educated or apprenticed to a family business were all obligations for a husband. A sum of money called the *mohar* had to be paid to the bride's father by the bridegroom before marriage. If necessary, the groom could partially pay this sum in the form of work, but the value of the mohar was returned to the daughter on the death of her parents, or if her husband died. The girl's father, in return for the mohar, gave her husband a wedding gift, or dowry, that might be in the form of money, servants, land, or property.

At the wedding ceremony, rings or bracelets were sometimes exchanged in a simple civil ceremony before two witnesses. The bride usually wore a veil and jewelry that included a traditional headband of ten coins. (Read more about such a wedding headband on pages 113–115.) The ceremony was then followed by a wedding feast at the home of the bridegroom, or his parents. All are familiar customs that are continued today in many parts of the world.

The marriage in Cana of Galilee is described in John 2:1–11. It was a large affair attended by Jesus, his mother, and several disciples. When the supply of wine ran low, Mary asked her son to intercede; he then performed the first of his miracles by turning water into wine. The incident shows not only the high regard that Jesus had for marriage, but the significance of customs and importance of wine at that time. It was a commodity of value, necessity, and tradition.

There are few references to the cost of goods and services during the life of Jesus, but some can be found in the New Testament, the Talmud, and the writings of Josephus. Daniel Sperber's book *Roman Palestine, 200–400: Money and Prices* (1974) gives many citations detailing wages and prices of that period. A loaf of bread, the staple midday lunch that was usually eaten with olives or fruit, cost one-eighth of a denarius. A full meal, including wine, was less than one denarius. A small amphora of wine, likely imported from Chios, also cost one denarius. Rent was about four denarii per month. The cost of some necessary religious offerings was equally modest.

> *Are not two sparrows sold for a small coin? Yet not one of them falls to the ground without your Father's knowledge. (Matthew 10:29)*

> *Are not five sparrows sold for two small coins? Yet not one of them has escaped the notice of God. (Luke 12:6)*

In the King James translation of these accounts, the word "farthing" is used to express the denomination of the coins involved in these examples. The farthing was the smallest English coin familiar to readers of the King James text. Other translations use the word *assarion*, a small Greek bronze coin that was equivalent to the Roman *as* and worth about 1/16 of a denarius. The original Latin text uses the words *asse* and *dipundio*, indicating similar denominations.

A bronze assarion from Chios in the first century B.C., with a sphinx seated on the obverse and a wine jar, called an amphora, on the reverse. This coin was identified as a "farthing" in the King James Bible. (Actual size approximately 18 mm.)

Jews were obligated to pay three different taxes. That due to the Roman emperors, paid in the form of Roman silver denarii, was at times used for the upkeep of heathen temples, which was offensive to the Jewish people. Those who collected the tax were despised because of their ruthless insistence on payment.

Silver coins of Tyre were the only money acceptable in the temple for payment of religious obligations. Didrachmas showing the head of Melkart, and an eagle, were equivalent to one-half shekel or two denarii. (Actual size approximately 21 mm.)

The redemption from priesthood tax was a religious tax, as was the temple tax used for temple repairs and other religious purposes. Jews everywhere, whether or not they lived in the land of Israel, were required to pay the annual one-half shekel temple tax. Exodus 30:13 references this tax as follows:

> *Every man age 20 or older paid a tax of a half shekel for the support of the tabernacle worship.*

ANCIENT LANGUAGES AND NAMES

Ever since the incident at the Tower of Babel, the meaning, pronunciation, and translation of words from one language to another has been a source of global confusion and misunderstanding. When one considers the changes in the English language over the past thousand years, or even the variations seen within our lifetime, it is easy to see the complexities created by language barriers. Today family names are often simplified or changed, and family lineage may be forgotten or disregarded. This is not simply a modern singularity, and it was undoubtedly the same with many people in biblical times. Various editions of the Bible have attempted to render the wording as closely as possible to the original text, or by using phrasing that can be best understood in modern vernacular.

Many names have been used to refer to Jesus. Was that his real name? What did his friends call him? Did he have a family name? What language did he speak? The answers are somewhat obscure in biblical passages, but it seems clear that Jesus must have spoken the common Aramaic language in everyday usage, and likely Hebrew when speaking in the temple. The name Jesus is an Anglicized version of *Yeshua*, and like many others at that time, he was most likely known as *Yeshua bar Yosef* (Jesus son of Joseph), or Jesus the Nazarene. The often-heard "Jesus Christ," is of course, not a family name, but an epitaph meaning "Jesus, the anointed one."

THE HOLY TEMPLE

The Holy Temple in Jerusalem was the epicenter of activity for nearly all things cultural and religious. The remains today are one of the most visited tourist attractions in the world, and they offer a thrilling, tangible personal connection to the daily life and the very paths the Prophets trod centuries ago.

The Second Temple was expanded and renovated by King Herod around 20 B.C., thus it was the center of all religious activity during the lifetime of Jesus, and the place where the faithful carried out their sacred duties. In Luke 2:22–24, we read where Mary and Joseph brought baby Jesus to the temple for the bris ceremony. As a grown man, he was often in the temple conversing with the elders, and answering their questions.

The Temple was destroyed during the Roman Siege of Jerusalem in A.D. 70.

Together, the existing remnants left behind from centuries past paint a vivid picture of what life was like through the ages, verifying the descriptions, lessons, and accounts recorded in biblical literature. A never-ending search for corroborating artifacts brings a special meaning and satisfaction to those who continue trying to more fully illuminate the past.

Chapter 6

Rulers of Judaea, 4 B.C. to A.D. 66

These were the men who governed in the Holy Land during roughly the first 70 years after the birth of Christ.

1. Ethnarch Archelaus
2. Coponius* (served under Emperor Augustus)
3. Marcus Ambibulus* (served under Emperor Augustus)
4. Annius Rufus
5. Valerius Gratus* (served under Emperor Tiberius)
6. Pontius Pilate* (served under Emperor Tiberius)
7. Marcellus
8. Marullus
9. Herod Agrippa I
10. Cuspius Fadus
11. Tiberius Alexander
12. Ventidius Cumanus
13. Antonius Felix* (served under emperors Claudius and Nero)
14. Porcius Festus* (served under Emperor Nero)
15. Lucceius Albinus
16. Gessius Florus

**Those with asterisks are the only ones known to have issued coins.*

Much of the daily life of the Jews was controlled by religious or governmental dictates. A number of religious groups or sects developed throughout the area. Most Jews did not belong to any sect, though those who did were widely admired. Among those sects were the Pharisees (the largest sect at the time of Jesus), the Hasidim (the "pious ones"), the Zealots (who refused to pay taxes to Rome), the Essenes (who possibly wrote the Dead Sea Scrolls), and the Sadducees (most of whom were members of the family of priests). The rabbis were teachers who interpreted the law and applied it to everyday life.

***The Pharisees and the Sadducees Come to Tempt Jesus*, James Tissot (c. 1886–1894).**

The procurators who ruled in Judaea governed under Roman authority, alongside the rulers of the Herodian dynasty and the governing body of the Sanhedrin. Not all of them issued coins, and few of them are remembered historically other than those mentioned in biblical or Roman texts, or those known to have issued coins. Pontius Pilate is the most famous because of his role in the trial of Jesus. Antonius Felix and Porcius Festus were governors during the trial of Paul.

HERODIAN COINS OF THE FIRST CENTURY A.D.

Herod Archelaus (4 B.C. to A.D. 6)

Herod Archelaus became ruler of Judaea upon the death of his father, Herod the Great. Raised and educated in Rome, the title of ethnarch was conferred upon him by Augustus. As the only prince of Judaea so named, his coins can be attributed with certainty. Archelaus ruled over the districts of Judaea, Idumaea, and Samaria. His coins are all undated and bear mainly maritime emblems, such as the prow, galley, and anchor, though other types feature the double cornucopia, a helmet, or a bunch of grapes. The main denomination was the prutah, but a double prutah was also issued.

The bronze prutot of Herod Archelaus, 4 B.C. to A.D. 6, varied in size and design. This son of Herod I ruled so harshly that he was hated by the Jews and removed from office by Augustus, who banished him to Gaul. (Actual size approximately 17 mm.)

When Joseph and Mary learned of the death of Herod the Great, they returned to the land of Israel. A reference to this incident is found in the New Testament.

> *When Herod had died, behold, the angel of the Lord appeared in a dream to Joseph in Egypt and said, "Rise, take the child and his mother and go to the land of Israel, for those who sought the child's life are dead." He rose, took the child and his mother, and went to the land of Israel. But when he heard that Archelaus was ruling over Judea in place of his father Herod, he was afraid to go back there, and because he had been warned in a dream, he departed for the region of Galilee, and came to dwell in a city called Nazareth. (Matthew 2:19–22)*

Herod Antipas (Tetrarch of Galilee, 4 B.C. to A.D. 39)

Herod Antipas began to issue coins only after he founded and settled his new capital, called Tiberias. His coins are all dated and were issued in several years beginning in A.D. 19/20, thus attesting to his long reign. Antipas was Herod the Great's original heir, but owing to disputes, a change of will gave him only Galilee and Peraea. The emblems on his coins are all of flora such as the reed, the palm branch, a small bunch of dates, and a palm tree.

Herod Antipas ruled under Tiberius and is mentioned in the Bible in several places. (Actual size approximately 19 mm.)

> *At that time Herod the tetrarch heard of the fame of Jesus. (Matthew 14:1)*

> *He replied, "Go and tell that fox, 'Behold, I cast out demons and I perform healings today and tomorrow, and on the third day I accomplish my purpose.'" (Luke 13:32)*

Antipas is the Herod who is so often mentioned in the New Testament after the Nativity story and was called "that fox" by Jesus. He ordered the execution of John the Baptist at the request of his wife, Herodias, after her daughter by an earlier marriage, Salome, had pleased Antipas with a dance.

> *But when Herod's birthday was kept, the daughter of Herodias (Salome) danced before them, and pleased Herod. (Matthew 14:6)*

> *For Herod himself had sent forth and laid hold upon John and bound him in prison, for Herodias' sake, his brother Philip's*

> *wife; for he had married her . . . and when the daughter of the said Herodias came in and danced, and pleased Herod . . . the king said unto the damsel, "Ask me whatsoever thou will . . ." and she came in . . . and asked saying, "I will that thou give me by and by, in a charger, the head of John the Baptist." (Mark 6:14–27)*

Jesus was sent to Herod Antipas by Pontius Pilate when it was found that he was a Galilean. Due to former disputes, Pilate was not on good terms with Herod. When the transfer of Jesus to the jurisdiction of Herod was made, the old quarrel with Pilate was ended. The incident is described in Luke 23:7–8 as follows:

> *Upon learning that he was under Herod's jurisdiction, he sent him to Herod who was in Jerusalem at that time. Herod was very glad to see Jesus; he had been wanting to see him for a long time, for he had heard about him and had been hoping to see him perform some sign.*

The convoluted life of Herod Antipas

Herod Antipas, also known Herod the Tetrarch, was married to Phasaelis, the daughter of Aretas IV. He divorced her in order to marry Herodias, the mother of Salome. Herodias was already married to his brother, Herod II. John the Baptist denounced the divorces as a violation of Mosaic law, setting the stage for his eventual beheading.

In the ensuing quarrel between King Aretas and Herod Antipas, a third brother, Philip the Tetrarch, assisted Aretas. Antipas was able to avoid capture only with the help of Roman forces, who came to his aid when he appealed to Emperor Tiberius.

In 2 Corinthians 11:32, the apostle Paul described how he had to quietly sneak out of Damascus by climbing through a window and being let down the wall in a basket to escape the clutches of King Aretas, who apparently was then in control of the Nabataean community in Damascus. Aretas died in A.D. 40 and was succeeded by his son Malichus II and daughter Shaqilath II.

Shown here is a copper coin of the Jewish tetrarch Herod Antipas and a first-century Nabataea copper coin of King Aretas IV with his second wife, Shaqilath. (Actual size c. 20 mm.)

Herod Philip I (4 B.C. to A.D. 34)

Herod Philip I is the least well-known son of Herod the Great. He was the first Jewish ruler to include his portrait on any coin, but the scarcity of his issues makes them elusive for collectors to acquire. His rejection of the Mosaic law against "graven images" was carried further by the representation of a Roman temple on the reverse of most of his coins. His coins were dated from the year 5 to the year 37 of his reign, though not all dates occur.

The portrait coins of Herod Philip are all quite rare. Luke (3:1) identifies him in the Bible as tetrarch of Ituraea. He ruled from 4 B.C. to A.D. 34 and issued coins in several denominations. (Actual size approximately 13 mm.)

> *Now in the fifteenth year of the reign of Tiberius Caesar, Pontius Pilate being governor of Judaea, and Herod being tetrarch of Galilee, and his brother Philip tetrarch of Ituraea and the region of Trachonitas . . . (Luke 3:1)*

King Herod Agrippa (A.D. 37–44)

King Herod Agrippa was the grandson of Herod the Great, and one of the best-recorded kings of ancient Israel. His life is chronicled in the Acts of the Apostles and in *Antiquities of the Jews* by Flavius Josephus. During his short time in office, he issued two distinct types of coins, of which bronze prutot made for Judaea in the sixth year of his reign (A.D. 42/43) are the most common. They depict an open umbrella, or royal canopy, on the obverse, and three ears of barley on the reverse; both inanimate designs were in keeping with Mosaic law. A parallel issue of Agrippa's coins was made for districts of his kingdom where his portrait or other Roman devices were not offensive. All of the portrait pieces are rare and seldom met with in coin collections.

Herod Agrippa ruled as king of Judaea from A.D. 37 to 44. He is remembered for the persecution of Christians and the execution of Apostle James. His prutah coins show a canopy or umbrella on the obverse and three ears of barley on the reverse. (Actual size approximately 17 mm.)

Agrippa is well known for his persecution of the early Christians, including killing James and imprisoning Peter.

> *About that time King Herod (Agrippa) laid hands upon some members of the church to harm them. He had James, the brother of John, killed by the sword, and when he saw that this was pleasing to the Jews he proceeded to arrest Peter also. (Acts 12:1–3)*

Salome and John the Baptist

Salome is described in the Gospels of Matthew 14 and Mark 6 as the daughter of Herodias, who asked Herod Antipas for the head of John the Baptist in return for her dance for the king.

Salome's name is also mentioned by Josephus in *Antiquities*, where he informs us that she married her great-uncle Philip the Tetrarch and, after Philip's death, her cousin Aristobulus, with whom she had three sons. Aristobulus was the son of Herod V of Chalcis and great-grandson of Herod I, and he was appointed king of Armenia Minor in the first year of Nero's reign. A rare portrait of him can be seen on some of his coins, along with that of Salome.

In the Gospel of Mark, Herodias is seen as being resentful of John for claiming that Herod's marriage to her was unlawful. When Salome danced before Herod at his birthday celebration, she was told that she could ask for anything she wanted as her reward. Salome's mother saw a chance to punish her accuser by requesting the head of the Baptist be brought to her on a platter.

Salome with the Head of John the Baptist, by Jan Adam Kruseman, c. 1861.

This Armenia Minor coin was struck in A.D. 66/67 (year 13 of Aristobulus's reign), the first year of the Jewish war and around 40 years after the execution of John the Baptist, which has been tentatively dated to sometime between 25 and 29 A.D. (Actual size 20 mm.)

But an opportunity came when Herod on his birthday gave a banquet for his nobles and military commanders and the leading men of Galilee. For when Herodias's daughter came in and danced, she pleased Herod and his guests. And the king said to the girl, "Ask me for whatever you wish, and I will give it to you." And he vowed to her, "Whatever you ask me, I will give you, up to half of my kingdom." And she went out and said to her mother, "For what should I ask?" And she said, "The head of John the Baptist." And she came in immediately with haste to the king and asked, saying, "I want you to give me at once the head of John the Baptist on a platter." And the king was exceedingly sorry, but because of his oaths and his guests he did not want to break his word to her. And immediately the king sent an executioner with orders to bring John's head. He went and beheaded him in the prison and brought his head on a platter and gave it to the girl, and the girl gave it to her mother. (Mark 6:21–28)

John the Baptist is further identified in Flavius Josephus's *Antiquities of the Jews* Book XVIII, Chapter 5, 1–2, as a prominent first-century figure:

Herod's army was destroyed by the treachery of some fugitives who though they were of the tetrarchy of Philip, joined with Herod's army. So Herod wrote about these affairs to Tiberius, who being very angry at the attempt made by Aretas, wrote to Vitellius to make war on him.

Now some of the Jews thought that the destruction of Herod's army came from God, and that very justly, as a punishment for what he did against John, that was called the Baptist, for Herod slew him, who was a good man, and commanded the Jews to execute virtue, both as to righteousness towards one another, and piety towards God, and so to come to baptism; for that the washing [with water] would be acceptable to him if they made use of it.

The death of St. John was commemorated on this silver 4 *tari* coin of Malta's Order of Knights of the Hospital of St. John of Jerusalem (Knights of Malta). It was issued by Giovanni Paolo Lascaris di Ventimiglia e Castellar, grandmaster, 1636–1657. (Actual size 32 mm.)

Herod of Chalcis (A.D. 41–48)

Herod of Chalcis was the brother of Agrippa I. He used the title "Friend of the Emperor" on his coins and included his portrait on all issues. All of his coins are very rare. Some are undated; others are dated "year three." When this Herod died in A.D. 48, the Roman Emperor Claudius assigned the province of Chalcis to his brother-in-law, Agrippa II. Herod of Chalcis's son, Aristobulus (A.D. 57–92), was married to the infamous Salome, who earlier had danced before Herod Antipas and demanded the head of John the Baptist.

Salome's lineage and her sinful conduct that triggered the beheading of John the Baptist are recorded in detail in Flavius Josephus's *Antiquities of the Jews*, in Book XVIII, Chapter 5, 4:

> *Herodias, was married to Herod [Philip], the son of Herod the Great, who was born of Mariamne the daughter of Simon the high priest, who had a daughter, Salome; after whose birth Herodias took upon her to confound the laws of our country, and divorced herself from her husband while he was alive, and was married to Herod [Antipas], her husband's brother by the father's side, he was tetrarch of Galilee, but her daughter Salome was married to Philip, the son of Herod, and tetrarch of Trachonitis; and as he died childless, Aristobulus the son of Herod, the brother of Agrippa, married her; they had three sons, Herod, Agrippa, and Aristobulus.*

Herod Agrippa II (A.D. 48–c. 98)

Herod Agrippa II issued the largest and most varied series of coins of the Herodians. Two types have his portrait. Others were issued at various mints and in five denominations. They were made in several years and with two different dating cycles. Some have the name of Nero in the legend. Collectors find these pieces an interesting and challenging series to study and collect. All are considered to be scarce and difficult to obtain, especially in choice condition.

Herod Agrippa II issued numerous different coins and denominations during his reign from A.D. 48–c. 98, but all of them are scarce and elusive. He disregarded the Jewish prohibition of graven images and included portraits on many of his coins. (Actual size approximately 18 mm.)

Agrippa II and his sister Bernice are best remembered in biblical reference by the following passage in the Acts of the Apostles 26:27–28.

> *"King Agrippa, do you believe the prophets? I know you believe." Then Agrippa said to Paul, "You will soon persuade me to be a Christian." Paul replied, "I would pray to God that sooner or later not only you but all who listen to me today might become as I am except for these chains." Then the king rose, and with him the governor and Bernice and the others who sat with them. After they had withdrawn they said to one another, "This man is doing nothing that deserves death or imprisonment" and Agrippa said to Festus, "This man could have been set free if he had not appealed to Caesar."*

The trial of Paul before Agrippa.

St. John the Baptist

One of the most famous, intriguing, and central figures to the birth of Christianity is John, the cousin of Jesus. From all accounts, the two were very close friends and allies in their resentment of Roman domination, hypocrisy, and various other evils of the day.

Accounts of John's holiness, Spartan lifestyle, and confrontation with Salome are so dramatic that they sound more like the plot of a modern novel or movie than a piece of biblical history. In fact, variations of the story have often made their way into both of those mediums.

John baptizes Jesus.

THE PROCURATORS OF JUDAEA

Herod Archelaus was banished to Vienna in 6 B.C. because of his cruelty to the Jews, and at that same time Judaea was annexed to the Roman province of Syria. Emperor Augustus then appointed Coponius to the post of prefect, or governor over Judaea. He was the first of 15 to hold the position of prefect or procurator and—with the exception of Agrippa I, who reigned as king—the procurators ruled there until the First Revolt of the Jews against Rome in A.D. 66. The coins of the procurators are identified by the emperors' regnal years that are printed on them, as the names of the procurators themselves do not appear on any coins.

Coponius (A.D. 6–9)

Coponius remained in office from A.D. 6 to 9, when he was recalled to Rome. He is not mentioned in the Bible but has been portrayed by

Flavius Josephus in *Antiquities* as being embroiled in the rivalry between Jews and Samaritans that flared up again during his tenure. His coins are easily found and relatively inexpensive. They are all small bronze prutot of a single design, that of an ear of barley with inscription in Greek on one side, and a palm tree with dates on the other. Lettering for the year 36 (of Augustus's reign) equate to A.D. 6.

The prutah coins of Coponius, A.D. 6–9, and those of Marcus Ambibulus, A.D. 9–12, are identical in design and can be distinguished only by the date on them. Jesus would have used these coins during his childhood. (Actual size approximately 16 mm.)

Marcus Ambibulus (A.D. 9–12)

Marcus Ambibulus succeeded Prefect Coponius and continued to issue coins of the same style and design: an ear of barley and a palm tree with two bunches of dates. His coins can be distinguished by the use of additional chronological dates for the reign of Emperor Augustus. The year 39 equals A.D. 9, 40 equates to A.D. 10, and 41 is A.D. 11. All were issued during the time that Jesus was growing up and would have been familiar to him.

Valerius Gratus (A.D. 15–26)

Valerius Gratus was sent from Rome by Tiberius to succeed Annius Rufus (who ruled Judaea from A.D. 12 to 15). He was prefect for 11 years, but little is known about him or his administration. There is no mention of Gratus in the Bible, although he must have been well known to all who lived in Judaea at that time. His coins are bronze prutot and a single lepton, with various designs including crossed cornucopias, lilies, vines with grapes, religious vessels, and palm branches. Following the custom of the day, his name does not appear on any of his coins, which often include the name of Tiberius Caesar and dates of his reign.

Valerius Gratus, who governed Judaea from A.D. 15 to 26, is not mentioned in the Bible, but his prutah coins circulated freely throughout the Holy Land. (Actual size approximately 15 mm.)

Pontius Pilate (A.D. 26–36)

Pontius Pilate is by far the best known of all administrators of this time. His existence, however, is not well documented by anything other than his coins. If it were not for his coins, and the biblical account of his delivery of Jesus to be crucified, he might well have gone unnoticed by historians. His approval by the Jews must have been tarnished by his lack of understanding or concern for their custom of excluding forbidden symbols on their coins.

Pontius Pilate, who governed for ten years, minted two different types of prutot in A.D. 29, 30, and 31. His role in history would have been relatively unknown it if were not for these coins and his part in the Crucifixion. (Actual size approximately 15 mm.)

Pilate issued only two types of coins during his ten-year term in office. The first bronze prutah is dated year 16 (of Tiberius Caesar) and was struck in A.D. 29. Its design includes three bound ears of barley on the obverse and the Roman sacrificial simpulum, or libation ladle, on the reverse. His second type of prutah shows an augur's wand, or lituus, on the obverse surrounded by Tiberius Caesar's name. The reverse has a date rendered in customary Greek letters indicating the year of Tiberius Caesar's reign: LIZ = 17 and LIH = 18. All of these are of special interest to collectors because Pilate issued them close to the year of the Crucifixion.

Pontius Pilate washing his hands after Jesus's fate has been decided.

When it was morning, all the chief priests and the elders of the people took counsel against Jesus to put him to death. They bound him, led him away, and handed him over to Pilate, the governor. (Matthew 27:1–2)

So Pilate went back into the praetorium and summoned Jesus and said to him, "Are you the King of the Jews?" Jesus answered, "Do you say this on your own or have others told you about me?" Pilate answered, "I am not a Jew, am I? Your own nation and the chief priests handed you over to me. What have you done?" (John 18:33–35)

Pilate said to them, "Then what shall I do with Jesus called Messiah?' They all said, 'Let him be crucified!" But he said, "Why? What evil has he done?" They only shouted the louder, "Let him be crucified!" When Pilate saw that he was not succeeding at all, but that a riot was breaking out instead, he took water and washed his hands in the sight of the crowd, saying, "I am innocent of this man's blood. Look to it yourselves." (Matthew 27:22–26)

When it was evening, there came a rich man from Arimathea named Joseph, who was himself a disciple of Jesus. He went to Pilate and asked for the body of Jesus; then Pilate ordered it to be handed over. (Matthew 27:57–58)

Antonius Felix (A.D. 52–60)

Antonius Felix served under the Roman Emperor Claudius for the first two years of his prefectship, then under Nero for his remaining term. In A.D. 54, when Britannicus ruled briefly with Nero, Felix issued a bronze prutah with the legend BPIT to recognize the young son of Claudius, who was subsequently poisoned by order of Nero. The reign of Felix was oppressive but strong. It was he who caused the apostle Paul to be sentenced to prison. A passage in the New Testament refers to this governor. When Paul was transferred to Caesarea from Jerusalem for his protection, a message was prepared to explain the mission:

And he wrote a letter after this manner: "Claudius Lysias unto the most excellent governor Felix, I send greeting." (Acts 23:26)

Apparently, Antonius Felix was not above accepting a bribe, as revealed in Acts 24:26, concerning the imprisonment of St. Paul:

He hoped also that money should have been given him of Paul, that he might loose him, wherefore he sent for him the oftener, and communed with him.

The coins of Felix consist of two different types of bronze prutot. Those under the authority of Claudius show crossed palm branches, while those made under Nero/Britannicus have crossed shields and spears. Both issues are dated year 14 of the reign of Caesar.

The apostle Paul was sentenced to prison by Antonius Felix, who served under Claudius in A.D. 52–54, and later under Nero in A.D. 54–62. Two different styles of prutah were made to recognize his Roman allegiances. (Actual size approximately 17 mm.)

Porcius Festus (A.D. 60–62)

Porcius Festus held the procuratorship under Nero for only about one year. He issued bronze prutot with the date LE (year 5), which equals A.D. 59, and Nero's name on the reverse. Paul was tried by Felix, but he was brought for judgment before Festus, who sent him to Rome. Paul was a Roman citizen and therefore was privileged to be tried and judged there. After two years in prison, Nero had Paul put to death. When Porcius Festus died in A.D. 61/62, Nero sent Albinus to succeed him. Reference to Festus is made in Acts 24:27 as follows:

> *But after two years, Porcius Festus came into Felix' room; and Felix, willing to show the Jews a pleasure, left Paul bound.*

Porcius Festus issued this bronze prutah in A.D. 59, near the time when he sentenced Paul to prison in Rome. (Actual size approximately 18 mm.)

The parable of the Good Samaritan.

Chapter 7

Coins in Parables, Lessons, and Stories

Coins and other forms of money were as central to daily life in first-century Israel as they are today, so it's no surprise that Jesus frequently used coins as a teaching tool when sharing parables and moral lessons. One of the most memorable of these parables concerns the laborers in a vineyard. The original Latin reference to the payment of a denarius a day for the workers gives confirmation of the standard wages of that time.

LABORERS IN THE VINEYARD

> *The kingdom of heaven is like a landowner who went out early in the morning to hire laborers for his vineyard. After agreeing with them for a denarius a day, he sent them into his vineyard. Going out about nine o'clock, he saw others standing idle in the marketplace, and he said to them, "You too go into my vineyard, and I will give you what is just."*
>
> *So they went. And again he went out again around noon, and around three o'clock, and did as before. Going out about five o'clock, he found others standing around, and said to them, "Why do you stand here idle all day?" They answered, "Because no one has hired us." He said to them, "You too go into my vineyard." When it was evening the owner of the vineyard said to his steward, "Call the laborers and give them their wages, beginning with the last and ending with the first."*
>
> *When those who had started about five o'clock came, each received a denarius. So when the first came, they thought that they would receive more, but they also received each his denarius. And on receiving it they began to grumbled against the landowner, saying, "These last ones worked only one hour, and you have made them equal to us, who bore the day's burden and the heat." He said to one of them in reply, "My friend, I am not cheating you. Did you not agree with me for a denarius? Take what is yours and go." (Matthew 20:1–15)*

Another reference to the familiarity of the Roman silver denarius in Jesus's time is found in the following passage: "A certain money-lender had two debtors; one owed five hundred denarii, the other fifty. As they had no means of paying, he forgave them both" (Luke 7:41–42). In this story, the creditor was a kind-hearted money-lender who forgave two debtors and was rewarded by their love and appreciation. The incident was extraordinary because it must have been a very unusual occurrence.

Luke recounts a very different story that Jesus preached when he spoke against hypocrisy and covetousness in another passage. In this, he mentions the "mite," the smallest coin in use at that time, and most likely a bronze lepton of the old Hasmonean era.

> *And when thou art going with thy opponent to the ruler, take pains to be quit of him on the way; lest he deliver thee to the judge, and the judge to the officer, and the officer cast thee into prison. I say to thee, thou wilt not come out from it until thou hast paid the very last mite. (Luke 12:58–59)*

THE LOST COIN

Some of the best-known parables have meanings that are not immediately recognized because they involve unfamiliar customs. The story of the "lost coin" is a classic example. In its simplest form, the woman who lost her coin would be expected to rejoice when it was found. But why would she call her friends together to celebrate with her? The answer lies in understanding why she was so concerned with the loss.

> *Or what woman, having ten drachmas, if she loses one drachma, does not light a lamp and sweep the house and search carefully until she finds it? And when she has found it, she calls together her friends and neighbors, saying, "Rejoice with me, for I have found the drachma that I had lost." (Luke 15:7–10)*

The key to more fully appreciating this parable lies in the number of coins that the woman had. The specific number of ten drachma coins is a clear reference to the headband that the woman wore to signify that she was married. It would have been a symbol equivalent to today's wedding ring, and precious to her for many reasons beyond its monetary value.

The mystery of the "lost coin" can be explained in understanding that the piece was part of a wedding headband and precious to the woman who lost it. Greek silver drachma coins and Roman denarii were often used for this custom. (Actual size approximately 18 mm.)

Ten Greek drachmas were the equivalent of ten denarii or ten days' pay—and a considerable sum of money—but beyond that, if a woman was found guilty of deception, one or more of the coins would be removed from the headband. In this story, the unfortunate woman who lost one of the coins was embarrassed to face her neighbors and friends for fear of being suspected of dishonesty and shameful behavior.

The use of Greek drachmas on the bridal headband was sometimes a part of a bride's dowry, and an old tradition for showing wealth and stability. It is a custom that has been used, with modifications, in some countries ever since. In ancient times, Roman silver denarii were used when the older Greek coins were not available. The coins were usually pierced with a nail and sewn onto the headband.

The Lost Coin was most likely one of the pierced pieces strung on a special headband. (Actual size 18mm.)

Whenever I read the parable of the Lost Coin, I reflect not only on why finding that coin was compared to the joy of recovering a repentant sinner. I also wonder what made the lowly coin so valuable, exactly what it was, and why precisely ten coins were mentioned. The original text is quite specific in calling the piece a *drachma*, a term that would have been a very familiar to Old Testament Greek and Hebrew people, but perhaps less so after Roman captivity when the *denarius* took its place as a coin of roughly the same size and value.

As a classic parable, it relates the story of recovery to a woman who, in the custom of the day, cherished her traditional headband of ten coins as a symbol of her marriage. While each was worth only approximately one day's wages, losing one also meant a loss of dignity and stability, and thus was of great value to her.

THE GOOD SAMARITAN

The denarius was mentioned in several other parables that confirm its familiarity to Jesus's audience. The story of the Good Samaritan was especially significant because of the animosity that usually existed between the Samaritans and the Jews.

A certain man was going down from Jerusalem to Jericho, and he fell in with robbers, who after both stripping him and beating him went their way, leaving him half-dead. But, as it happened, a certain priest was going down the same way; and when he saw him, he passed by. And likewise a Levite also, when he was near the place and saw him, passed by. But a certain Samaritan as he journeyed came upon him, and seeing him, was moved with compassion. And he went up to him and bound up his wounds, pouring on oil and wine. And setting him on his own beast, he brought him to an inn and took care of him. And the next day he took out two denarii and gave them to the innkeeper. (Luke 10:30–35)

Roman silver denarii, like these of Octavian (Augustus) and Tiberius, could have been among the coins that were given to the innkeeper by the Good Samaritan for the care of a wounded Jewish man.

The Samaritans claimed descent from a group of Israelites from the tribes of Ephraim and Manasseh. They were treated badly by the Romans while under their jurisdiction and were despised by the Jewish community, possibly because of the Samaritans' firm conviction that theirs was the true religion of the ancient Israelites. Aside from the parable about assisting a wounded traveler, the Samaritans are also mentioned in 2 Chronicles 36:22–23, where the Persian emperor Cyrus the Great (559–530 B.C.) permitted the return of exiles to their homeland and ordered the rebuilding of the Temple of Jerusalem.

MONEYCHANGERS IN THE TEMPLE

> *And Jesus entered the temple of God, and cast out all those who were selling and buying in the temple, and he overturned the tables of the moneychangers and the seats of those who sold the doves. And he said to them, "It is written, 'My house shall be called a house of prayer [Isaiah 56:7; Jeremiah 7:11]; but you have made it a den of thieves.'" (Matthew 21:12–13)*

> *And he found in the Temple those who were selling oxen and sheep and doves, and the moneychangers seated. (John 2:14)*

This famous story of Jesus's life concerns the habit of merchants setting up stalls in the outer court of the temple. There they sold sacrificial animals and offered to change foreign money into the acceptable Tyrian shekels and minor copper coins of the old Hasmonean rulers.

Mosaic law forbade charging interest on loans to fellow Jews, but the moneychangers took advantage of their unique position by adding a fee of about eight percent for their services.

Moneychangers in the temple converted "heathen" money to acceptable Tyrian and Maccabean coins. The fee for their services was seen as an offense to the pious Jews. A silver tetradrachm of Ptolemy III, c. 230 B.C., showing the king's image, would have been converted to a similar piece from Tyre. (Actual size approximately 28 mm.)

Large transactions usually involved gold coins similar to the staters of Philip II (359–336 B.C.) that show the head of Apollo and a racing chariot. (Actual size approximately 18 mm.)

They have taken gifts in thee to shed blood: thou has taken usury and increase, and covetously oppressed thy neighbors: and then has forgotten me, says the Lord God. (Ezekiel 22:12)

Take not usury of him nor more than you have given: fear thy God, that thy brother may live with thee. (Leviticus 25:36)

THE WIDOW'S MITE

> *And Jesus sat down opposite the treasury, and observed how the crowd were putting money into the treasury; and many rich people were putting in large sums. And there came one poor widow, and she put in two mites, which make a quadrans. And he called his disciples together, and said to them, "Amen I say to you, this poor widow has put in more than all those who have been putting money into the treasury. For they all have put in out of their abundance; but she out of her want has put in all that she had—all that she had to live on."* (Mark 12:41–44)

> *But looking up he saw the rich who were putting their gifts into the treasury. And he saw also a certain poor widow putting in two mites. And he said, "Truly I say to you, this poor widow has put in more than all."* (Luke 21:1–4)

In another well-known parable, as told in the Gospels of Mark and Luke, the poor widow contributes what is described as two "mites." All accounts emphasize that the mite was the smallest bronze coin in use at that time. Although there is no coin known by that name, it is logical to assume that the passage refers to the tiny lepta from the time of Alexander Jannaeus, the second king of the Hasmonean dynasty. Although those coins were made approximately 100 years earlier, they were still being used in the temple as offerings. Lepta of Jannaeus were the smallest of all Hasmonean coins and the most plentiful in ancient times, just as they are today. Collectors treasure them because they are so closely connected to a biblical incident, and so readily available.

The coins that the poor widow gave to the temple were small lepta, or "mites," which represented much of her sustenance.

According to this parable, each of the two lepta was worth one-half of a Roman quadrans, which was a small bronze coin. There were 64 quadrans to the denarius, and thus her total offering was about equivalent to 1/64 of a day's wages. The miniscule sum was more than she could afford and offers a poignant lesson in selfless giving.

THE COIN IN THE FISH'S MOUTH

> *And when they had come to Capharnum, those who were collecting the didrachma came to Peter, and said, "Does your Master not pay the didrachma?" He said, "Yes." But when he had entered the house, Jesus spoke first, saying, "What dost thou think, Simon? From whom do the kings of the earth receive tribute or customs; from their own sons, or from others?" And he said, "From others." Jesus said to him, "The sons then are exempt. But that we may not give offense to them, go to the sea and cast a hook, and take the first fish that comes up. And opening its mouth thou wilt find a stater; take that and give it to them for me and for thee." (Matthew 17:23–26)*

The money mentioned in the Latin rendition of this parable is more exacting than that of the usual translations. In the King James Version, and other accounts, we find the coin referred to as "a piece of money." All agree that the coin retrieved from the fish was the size of a tetradrachm, or shekel, because that was the necessary amount to pay the tax for two people. The term "stater" referred to a Greek coin that was approximately equal to the tetradrachm, and twice the value of the half-shekel tax.

Jesus found money for tribute in a most unlikely place: a fish's mouth. The coin must have been a tetradrachm of Tyre, the exact amount needed to pay the tax for Peter and himself.

Finding such a coin in the mouth of a fish was miraculous, but not unnatural. Perhaps the fish Peter reeled in was a variety of the African mouthbrooding cichlids. They have the unusual habit of holding eggs in their mouth for protection during incubation. It could have been a natural instinct for such a fish to retrieve a shiny lost coin and hold it in its mouth.

THE TRIBUTE PENNY

> *Then the Pharisees went and took counsel how they might trap him in his talk. And they sent to him their disciples, with the Herodians, saying, "Master, we know that thou art truthful, and that thou teachest the way of God in truth and that thou carest naught for any man; for thou dost not regard the person of men. Tell us, therefore, what dost thou think: Is it lawful to give tribute to Caesar, or not?" But Jesus, knowing their wickedness, said "Why do you test me, you hypocrites? Show me the coin of the tribute." So they offered him a denarius. Then Jesus said to them, "Whose are this image and the inscription?" They said to him, "Caesar's." Then he said to them, "Render, therefore, to Caesar the things that are Caesar's, and to God the things that are God's." And hearing this they marveled, and leaving him went off. (Matthew 22:15–22)*

The Pharisees and Herodians conspire together against Jesus.

The question, the answer, and the moral of this story seem simple and clear. Even the coin that is mentioned is easy to identify when it is called a denarius. The Roman census tax at that time was one denarius, the equivalent of one day's pay. The King James Bible uses the word "penny" in place of denarius in order to make the word more understandable to sixteenth-century readers who were familiar with the English silver penny, which was approximately the same size as the old Roman silver coin. Throughout the years this story has become so well known that the Roman denarius of Tiberius has become widely known as "the Tribute Penny."

When the Pharisees attempted to trap Jesus into betraying his duty to God or to Caesar, he called for a denarius to show that it was issued by Caesar. Such coins show a portrait of the Roman emperor on the obverse, and his mother Livia on the reverse. (Actual size approximately 20 mm.)

It is popularly believed that the coin involved was a Roman silver denarius of Emperor Tiberius (ruled A.D. 14–37) or Caesar Augustus (ruled 27 B.C.–A.D. 14), which would have featured the ruler's image and an inscription of his name. However, researcher Danny Syon of the Israel Antiquities Authority has written that denarii of both of these rulers are not commonly found in Israel. He believes the coin was more likely bronze, with a portrait of either Augustus or Tiberius, which was enhanced to be a denarius when the story was later written. Tiberius, known as Caesar, ruled from A.D. 14 to 37, during the lifetime of Jesus, and his coins would have been in use throughout Judaea at that time. They would also have been required for payment of the census or tax. A similar coin of Caesar Augustus (27 B.C.–A.D. 14) could also have been used, but there is widespread accord about the coin of Tiberius being the specific piece.

As straightforward as this story seems, it has much deeper significance than is at first apparent. The Herodians who accompanied the Pharisees were there to see if Jesus would be disloyal to his obligation to pay the Roman tax. If he did, he surely would have been accused of being an enemy of Rome. The Pharisees were there to see if Jesus would betray his Jewish allegiance. Either answer, it seemed, would alienate him to one group or the other. It was a trap from which, they believed, he could not escape.

The answer that Jesus gave to his adversaries was brilliant and disarming. "Repay to Caesar what belongs to him"—that is, those who willingly used Caesar's coins should repay him in kind. The answer avoided taking sides in the question of the lawfulness of the tax. Those who hypocritically asked about duty to the law of God were told to be concerned with what is due to God.

OTHER STORIES OF MONEY

The New Testament speaks of the use of money in various ways. The gold coins cited in the parable of the Gold Pieces, as recorded by Luke, were possibly Greek staters of Alexander the Great, or Roman aurei of Augustus or Tiberius worth 25 denarii each.

> *A certain nobleman went into a far country to obtain for himself a kingdom and then return. And having summoned ten of his servants, he gave them ten gold pieces and said to them, "Trade till I come." (Luke 19:12–13)*

The Roman denarii—or, in some translations, the more generic "silver coins"—also appear in the parable of the Unmerciful Servant, who is treated with mercy by his master but punished for being unforgiving to the man who owed him.

> *But as that servant went out, he met one of his fellow-servants who owed him a hundred denarii, and he laid hold of him and throttled him, saying, "Pay what you owe." (Matthew 18:28–30)*

The Gospel of John also tells of a woman pouring an expensive perfume, worth about a year's wages, over Jesus's feet prior to his crucifixion. The value of the perfume prompted Judas Iscariot to object to its use, though Jesus rebukes him.

> *Why was this ointment not sold for three hundred denarii, and given to the poor? (John 12:5)*

Chapter 8

Tetradrachms and Treachery

THIRTY PIECES OF SILVER

The term "pieces of silver" is used many times in the Bible in reference to coins, or pieces called hacksilber, that were equivalent in weight to the shekel. The tetradrachms of Tyre were coins that had been approved for use as offerings in the temple and were the most commonly available coins in use throughout the Holy Land. They were relatively large coins for that time and had a value of nearly four days' pay. Although these coins contained only about a half ounce of silver, we must remember that ancient coins had a purchasing power far greater than today, and a single shekel was considered to be a significant sum of money.

There were established prices for the value of a life in ancient times, as is shown in both the Old and New Testaments.

> *If the ox gore a bondman or a handmaid, he shall give to their master thirty shekels of silver, and the ox shall be stoned. (Exodus 21:32)*

> *And when the Madianite merchants passed by, they drew him out of the pit, and sold him to the Ismaelites, for twenty pieces of silver, and they led him into Egypt. (Genesis 37:28)*

> *And I bought her to me for fifteen pieces of silver, and for a core of barley, and for half a core of barley. (Hosea 3:2)*

> *Then was fulfilled that which was spoken by Jeremiah the prophet, saying: And they took the thirty pieces of silver, the price of him that was prized, whom they prized of the children of Israel. (Matthew 27:9)*

Judas receives his silver for the betrayal of Jesus.

A fixed "blood-price" was not without precedent. Many other cultures throughout time have set similar standards for practical purposes. The custom seems more sophisticated than the current practice of arbitrarily placing the value of a life in millions of dollars, as seen in some lawsuits.

The price that was agreed upon for the betrayal of Jesus was the usual price of a life taken by accident or that of a slave being sold into captivity. It would equate to about 120 days' pay, or approximately what one would spend for five months' living expenses. There could be no justification for any amount of money given in exchange for such a life, but in that time and place, it was a standard value.

> *Then one of the Twelve, called Judas Iscariot, went to the chief priests, and said to them, "What are you willing to give me for delivering him to you?" And they assigned him thirty pieces of silver. And from then on he sought out an opportunity to betray him. (Matthew 26:15–16)*

> *Then Judas, who delivered him up, seeing that he had been condemned, filled with remorse, returned the thirty pieces of silver to the chief priests and the elders . . . And having cast down the pieces of silver in the temple, he left the place, and went away and hanged himself. And the chief priests took the pieces of silver and said, "It is not lawful to cast them into the treasury, since it is the price of blood." (Matthew 27:3, 5–6)*

There is little doubt that the coins given to Judas Iscariot were shekels from the Phoenician city of Tyre. A few other coins of the same weight could have been included in the payment, because they were not intended to be used in the temple, but the availability of the Tyrian coins makes them the number one candidate for this momentous transaction.

Judas Iscariot agreed to betray Jesus for 30 pieces of silver. The coins were quite likely tetradrachms of Tyre that had recently been made in Jerusalem, similar to this one minted in A.D. 10. The amount was a considerable sum in purchasing power at the time. (Actual size approximately 26 mm.)

Tyrian coins were accepted by the Jewish community despite their depiction of an eagle and a foreign god. The obverse of these coins shows the head of Melkart with a lion's skin around his neck and a laurel wreath on his head. He was a Phoenician god, shown posing in the form of the Greek god Herakles. On the reverse is an eagle standing on the prow of a ship, carrying a palm under its right wing. In the field are letters and symbols indicating the date in which these coins were minted, from 126/125 B.C. to the time of the First Revolt of the Jews against Rome.

Jesus stands before Pontius Pilate in their first interview.

PONTIUS PILATE

The betrayal, crucifixion, and death of Jesus are related in Matthew 27 and John 18. Pontius Pilate becomes a central figure in this scenario, where the arrest and trial of Jesus are described in some detail.

> *Pilate therefore went outside to them, and said, "What accusation do you bring against this man?" They said to him in answer, "If he were not a criminal, we should not have handed him over to you." Pilate therefore said to them, "Take him yourselves, and judge him according to your law." The Jews then said to him, "It is not lawful for us to put anyone to death." (John 18:29–31)*

Pilate was a minor administrator who might well have been forgotten if it was not for his involvement in the trial of Jesus. He is mentioned in the New Testament, but the only other solid evidence of his existence lies in the bronze prutot that he minted in years near to the Crucifixion. One of these is dated LIZ (year 17), indicating A.D. 30, and possibly the year that Jesus died. The others were made in the years 16 and 18. The two designs Pilate used both bear the name of the emperor Tiberius Caesar rather than that of Pilate.

Some of the bronze lepta coins of Pontius Pilate were minted in years close to the crucifixion. The exact date of the event is not known for certain, but it could have been the year 17 of Pilate's coins, or A.D. 30. (Actual size approximately 15 mm.)

> *Pilate said to them, "Then what shall I do with Jesus called Messiah?" They all said, "Let him be crucified!" But he said, "Why? What evil has he done?" They only shouted the louder, "Let him be crucified!" When Pilate saw that he was not succeeding at all, but that a riot was breaking out instead, he took*

water and washed his hands in the sight of the crowd, saying, "I am innocent of this man's blood. Look to it yourselves." And the whole people said in reply, "His blood be upon us and upon our children." Then he released Barabbas to them, but after he had Jesus scourged, he handed him over to be crucified. (Matthew 27:22–26)

CASTING LOTS FOR HIS GARMENTS

The soldiers therefore, when they had crucified him, took his garments and divided them into four shares, a share for each soldier. They also took his tunic, but the tunic was seamless, woven in one piece from the top down. So they said to one another, "Let us not tear it, but cast lots for it to see whose it will be," in order that the passage of scripture might be fulfilled: "they divided my garments among them, and for my vesture they cast lots." This is what the soldiers did. (John 19:23–24)

A Roman fresco from Pompeii of a dice game.

And after they had crucified him, they divided his garments, casting lots, that it might be fulfilled which was spoken by the prophet, saying: "They divided my garments among them; and upon my vesture they cast lots." (Matthew 27:35)

Throwing dice, or casting lots, was a widespread and normal part of life in New Testament times. Games were played with lots, much as dice are still used, but the pieces were slightly different in that they were marked only on two or four sides. The pieces could be made of bone, wood, or even bronze.

The six-sided dice originated several thousand years ago. They were popularly used by many civilizations, including the Romans, just as they are used in a variety of games today.

The contest played by the soldiers at the crucifixion, as recorded by John and Matthew, was a game that used Roman dice. This would have been in favor of simply "matching coins," another favorite pastime of the soldiers. If bronze pieces were used, they were just as valuable as coins because all metal items were highly prized at that time. The large Roman copper shipbuilder's nails that may have been used at the Crucifixion would also have been as valuable as money.

Large copper shipbuilder's nails were sometimes used to affix criminals to a post or cross in the torturous execution known as crucifixion. (Actual size approximately 95 mm.)

Roman Crucifixion

A graphic account of the horrific crucifixion of Jesus is narrated in several of the gospels of Matthew, Mark, Luke, and John. Details of the procedure and nature of this despicable act have also been recorded in various other descriptions of the ancient Roman custom.

Punishment for serious offenses has been carried out in many ways, but by all accounts, crucifixion was one of the most horrendous. Its very intent was to inflict the maximum amount of humiliation and pain for the longest possible time before the victim died.

Under Roman law, this method of execution was normally used only for slaves, foreigners, revolutionaries, and the worst criminals. Most Roman citizens were exempt from crucifixion, except in the case of desertion from military service. Flogging was a legal preliminary to every Roman execution, and only women and Roman senators, or faithful soldiers, were exempt.

The flogging whip was usually short and made of braided leather strips, which were often imbedded with shreds of metal or bone that tore the flesh with each lash. For scourging, a man was stripped of his clothing and tied to an upright post. The Gospel accounts indicate that Jesus was severely whipped and imply that the scourging was particularly harsh. It is unknown whether the number of lashes was limited to 39, in accordance with Jewish law.

Criminals condemned to crucifixion often had to carry part of their cross to the place of execution. This normally would be the large crossbeam to which they would be affixed by any number of painful methods, sometimes by being nailed or strangled with ropes, until they eventually died from exhaustion or asphyxiation.

Several variations of a cross were used, no doubt depending on whatever was available. Lumber of any sort was a scarce and valuable commodity. The often-seen image of a huge, tall cross with a massive crossbeam more likely comes from the imagination of fourth-century artists trying to convey the event's magnitude. A simple X-shaped gibbet was often used, as was any available tree.

According to Roman law, at the site of execution, the victim was given a drink of wine mixed with gall as a mild pain reliever. His hands could then be nailed or tied to the crossbars, but nailing was usually preferred by Roman executioners. Common copper shipbuilder's nails were frequently

chosen because of their ease of use and value after being retrieved and divided among the executioners. Copper was a desirable commodity and used in ship construction because of its resistance to rust.

The hand-forged nails that were used were normally 3 to 4 inches long. Their square shape, taper, and characteristic wide dome-shaped head are easily recognizable from specimens known today. While nails could be used to immobilize hands, they were more efficiently used to secure the wrist, where they would support the weight of the body and cause the most pain by penetrating nerves.

And when they came to the place that is called The Skull, there they crucified him, and the criminals, one on his right and one on his left. And Jesus said, "Father, forgive them, for they know not what they do." And they cast lots to divide his garments. And the people stood by, watching, but the rulers scoffed at him, saying, "He saved others; let him save himself, if he is the Christ of God, his Chosen One!" The soldiers also mocked him, coming up and offering him sour wine and saying, "If you are the King of the Jews, save yourself!" (Luke 23:33–43)

And they brought him to the place called Golgotha (which means Place of a Skull). And they offered him wine mixed with myrrh, but he did not take it. And they crucified him and divided his garments among them, casting lots for them, to decide what each should take. And it was the third hour when they crucified him. And the inscription of the charge against him read, "The King of the Jews." (Mark 15:22–32)

And about the ninth hour Jesus cried out with a loud voice, saying, "Eli, Eli, lema sabachthani?" that is, "My God, my God, why have you forsaken me?" (Matthew 27:46)

Some women were watching from a distance. Among them were Mary Magdalene, Mary the mother of James the younger and of Joseph, and Salome. In Galilee these women had followed him and cared for his needs. Many other women who had come up with him to Jerusalem were also there. (Mark 15:40–41)

Crucifixion as Reported in Other Sources

Additional commentary on the practice of crucifixion can be found in the writings of the contemporary historian Flavius Josephus in *Antiquities of the Jews*, **in what is considered a prime source of literary information about punishment bestowed on the disobedient. Josephus says in** *Antiquities* **12, Chapter 5, that criminals were "whipped with rods, and their bodies were torn to pieces, and were crucified, while they were still alive." Josephus was a general in command of the Jewish forces of Galilee during the First Revolt against Rome, in the middle of the first century, and reported directly to the Roman General Titus. Thus, he was well acquainted with the custom.**

In *Antiquities* 18, Chapter 3, Josephus details the conflicts between the Romans and the Jews and their attempts to preserve their customs and faith. It presents a vivid history of life in first-century Judaea. My copy of *The Genuine Works of Josephus*, and *Antiquities of the Jews*, is a translation of the original by William Whiston, printed in Edinburgh in 1794. Unfortunately, it contains some additions that refer to Jesus being crucified, which are considered to be understandings by the translator and not the true original text. Therefore, I will not include them here, although they do contain some interesting reading. The balance of the narrative, however, contains reliable historical data.

SOLDIERS AT THE TOMB

When Jesus was laid to rest in the tomb, Roman soldiers were posted there to guard against the body being stolen, so that the disciples could say their Lord had risen. An account of the Resurrection is given in the Gospels of Matthew, Mark, Luke, and John. All are in accord about the holy women carrying spices to the sepulcher and reaching it after sunrise; they are anxious about the heavy stone, but know nothing of the official guard. In Matthew 28:2–4, an angel frightens the guards, puts them to flight, and rolls away the stone.

A first-century tomb near Nazareth.

> *Now while they were going, behold, some of the guard came into the city and reported to the chief priests all that had happened. And when they had assembled with the elders and had consulted together, they gave much money to the soldiers, telling them, "Say, his disciples came by night and stole him while we were sleeping. And if the procurator hears of this, we will persuade him and keep you out of trouble." And they took the money, and did as they were instructed. (Matthew 28:11–15)*

The money that the soldiers received as a bribe for their silence has been described as a large sum, indicating that the coins might have been either Tyrian shekels or perhaps a Roman gold aureus of Emperor Tiberius.

Soldiers were bribed to deny that Jesus had risen from the tomb on the first Easter morning. A gold aureus (equal to 25 silver denarii) of Roman Emperor Tiberius might have been part of the payment. The design on these coins was the same as on his denarii. (Actual size approximately 20 mm.)

Martyrdom in the early Christian church.

Chapter 9

The Development and Spread of Christianity

REVOLTS OF THE JEWS AGAINST ROME

While Nero's actions launched centuries of persecution against the Christians, his excesses also extended to Jerusalem, where his oppression of the Jews caused a major revolt in A.D. 66. In 67 Nero appointed Vespasian, a skillful military leader, to quell the rebellion. He was proclaimed emperor of Rome soon after Nero's death, and his eldest son Titus successfully ended the war in A.D. 70. Vespasian's victories in Jerusalem afforded him a military distinction that was reflected in his coinage, which often depicted the defeated Jews with the inscription JUDAEA CAPTA. Some of his insulting coins also show a sow with piglets, the insignia of the 10th Legion sent to Jerusalem to quell the uprising. Upon Vespasian's deathbed, he is reported to have said, "Alas, I think I am becoming a god." Soon after, the Senate deified him, but the honor was more akin to sainthood than the actual elevation to a god's status.

Vespasian quelled the Jewish uprising in Jerusalem in A.D. 70 and issued many coins to commemorate his victory. A typical design shows Judaea seated beneath a trophy, with the legend "Judaea Capta." (Actual size approximately 19 mm.)

One of the most detested victory coins of Vespasian is a denarius showing a pig and piglets on the reverse, as an insult to the Jews. (Actual size approximately 19 mm.)

Throughout the revolution that lasted from A.D. 66 to 70, a large number of purely Jewish coins were made to supply the needs of war, as offerings for the temple, and as political or inspirational statements. These were all special coins made with religiously acceptable designs, such as a bronze prutah that displayed a grape leaf on one side and an amphora, or jar, on the other. The legend on these coins reads "For the freedom of Zion," and a reference to the year of issue, either year two or three of the revolution.

It was during this time that the famous Jewish shekel coins were first made. Before this, any biblical reference to a shekel indicated a

A replica of a Roman milestone, on exhibit at the Diaspora Museum in Tel Aviv. The original milestone was found near Shahhat, Libya, and was erected in the time of Emperor Hadrian. The inscription on the milestone reads: "The Emperor Caesar son of the late Trajan who vanquished the Parthians, grandson of the late Nerva Trajan Hadrian Augustus, the high priest, serving as tribune for the second term and as consul for the third, has repaved the road which was overturned and shattered in the Jewish revolt."

weight of approximately one-half ounce, or the equivalent silver tetradrachm of Tyre, that had been authorized for use as a religious offering. The revolt gave opportunity and incentive for the Jewish leaders to issue a coin of their own that would show their independence and resolve, as well as suiting their commitment to using money without a graven image. The issuance of these Jewish coins was also necessitated by the discontinuation of old Tyrian-style shekels around A.D. 65.

A typical bronze coin of the First Revolt period has a ceremonial cup on the obverse and a vine leaf on the reverse. (Actual size approximately 17 mm.)

The silver shekel and half-shekel coins that were produced during the period of the First Revolt share a common design, with a ceremonial cup on the obverse and three pomegranates on the reverse. The Hebrew legend on these coins contains the date (one through five), the denomination (shekel, or half-shekel, of Israel), and "Jerusalem the Holy." The silver shekels weigh approximately 14 grams, and the half-shekel coins weigh approximately 7 grams. All of these coins are thick and clumpy, with edges that have been hammered, or peened.

The famous shekel of the Bible was not an actual coin until such pieces were made by the rebelling Jews in A.D. 66–70. The design of these shekels and half-shekels shows a ceremonial cup on the obverse and three pomegranates on the reverse. (Actual size approximately 23 mm.)

***The Siege and Destruction of Jerusalem by the Romans Under the Command of Titus, A.D. 70,* David Roberts (1850).**

In the devastating revolutionary war that lasted for more than four years, the Roman emperor Vespasian and his son Titus destroyed much of Jerusalem, including the Holy Temple, and killed tens of thousands of citizens. The Roman 10th and 12th legions slowly, but surely, quelled the revolt and brought the situation back under their control. The Jewish historian Josephus recorded that the total number of prisoners taken during the war amounted to 97,000 and those who perished during the entire siege numbered more than a million. Reference to this is found in Isaiah 3:26 as follows: "And her gates shall lament and mourn, and she shall sit desolate on the ground."

The Roman 10th Legion was sent to Jerusalem to fight in the Jewish War. Many bronze coins were counterstamped with the Roman numeral X to indicate their presence during the sieges of Jerusalem and Masada. (Actual size approximately 29 mm.)

THE UPRISINGS UNDER TRAJAN

Emperor Trajan (98–117) sought to solidify his empire and ensure a degree of peaceful coexistence during his reign. In Laodicea ad Mare, a seaport of Syria south of Antioch, commerce flourished under the Romans. The Laodiceans were ordered to allow their Jewish fellow citizens to celebrate the Sabbath and to practice their other religious observances. Saint Paul, the earliest known Christian author, wrote several letters (or epistles) to various churches, and in one he stated, "After this letter has been read to you, see that it is also read in the church of the Laodiceans."

This Syrian bronze coin from Laodicea ad Mare was issued by Trajan in A.D. 114/115. The obverse shows a bust of Emperor Trajan. On the reverse is a city goddess.

Roman silver denarius of Trajan.

In an effort to unify the eastern borders of his empire, in 115 Trajan attacked Armenia and the kingdom of the Syrian Parthians. Believing he had been victorious, he was surprised when several Messianic revolts broke out simultaneously. Fearing that the revolt would spread to the Jews in the eastern provinces, Trajan had his general, Lusius Quietus, organize a force to kill many Cypriot, Mesopotamian, and Syrian Jews. These suppressive efforts only exacerbated the friction between the Romans and Jews, including those of the newly formed sect known as Jewish Christians.

Between the years of 115 and 117, full-fledged hostilities broke out in what has been called the "War of Quietus." It was fought mostly in Cyrenaica, Cyprus, Egypt, and Mesopotamia. The revolts were a direct result of the oppressive reign of Domitian, who was especially hard on Jews and Christians, as well as attacks under Trajan's rule on both Jewish and Christian leaders.

The cavalry of Lucius Quietus fighting the Dacians, as depicted on Trajan's Column.

During Trajan's Parthian campaign from 115 to 116, Quietus sacked the cities of Nisibis and Edessa and suppressed revolts in Babylonia. Major revolts by the Jews in Cyrene, Cyprus, Mesopotamia, and Egypt resulted in the ransacking of towns and the slaughter of Roman citizens by Jewish rebels. Quietus took the city of Lydda and soon defeated the rebels. As his reward, in 117 Quietus was appointed governor of Palestine and given unlimited power. While the crucial Jewish insurrections at this time were outside of Judaea, it is quite probable that the restlessness in Judaea at the time was the precursor to the Bar Kokhba War, which erupted 14 years later. By 117, failing health and the stress of the Jewish uprising had forced Trajan to abandon his project, and he died in Cilicia on his way back to Rome.

BAR KOKHBA'S WAR

The second revolt of the Jews against Rome was under the leadership of Simon Bar Kokhba. It lasted from A.D. 133 to 135 and was the occasion for minting the last Jewish coins in antiquity. The inscriptions on these coins contain the name Shimeon (Simon) and sometimes his title "Prince of Israel," and other coins of the period bear the name of "Eleazar the Priest," or simply "Jerusalem." Bar Kokhba coins of the first two years were dated "Year one of the redemption of Israel," or "Year two of the freedom of Israel." During the third year and until the end of the war, the coins were undated and bore the slogan "For the freedom of Jerusalem."

The entrance to a cave used by the Bar Kokhba rebels.

The revolt of 132 was sparked by continued harassment from the Roman emperors, particularly Hadrian, who intended to rebuild Jerusalem and rename it Aelia Capitolina. He also passed laws that forbade circumcision under the penalty of death. Under the leadership of Bar Kokhba, the resistance fighters made a heroic effort to oust the Romans in the hopes of rebuilding their own city and the Holy Temple that was central to their religion. In this role Bar Kokhba was seen by some as the promised Messiah, and greatly revered. His name, which means "son of a star," was even foretold by prophecy: "There shall step forth a star (kokhba) out of Jacob, And a scepter shall rise out of Israel." (Numbers 24:17). Proof of his existence, however, was only told by his coins until papyrus containing letters from him were found in the Dead Sea caves in 1960 and 1961.

Coins that were minted during the Bar Kokhba War were made of silver and bronze, and in many different designs. The entire issue was overstruck on older coins that were taken from circulation around the district of Palestine. These included Roman provincial tetradrachms from Antioch, the ubiquitous Roman denarii, provincial drachmas, and local bronze city coins, mainly from Ashkelon and Gaza. It is believed that Bar Kokhba possibly obtained the Gentile coins needed for overstriking by means of a public loan for the war effort.

A second revolt of the Jews against the Romans occurred in A.D. 132. It was brought about by Emperor Hadrian, who enacted laws forbidding religious activities under penalty of death. His silver denarii show the emperor's portrait. (Actual size approximately 19 mm.)

A new type of shekel, or sela, was minted during the Second Revolt from A.D. 132 to 135. These silver coins are attributed to Simon Bar Kokhba and have various dates and legends. The central image is a frontal view of the temple. (Actual size approximately 26 mm.)

Bronze coins of the Second Revolt were made in several different sizes and designs. The most prevalent coins show a palm tree on the obverse and a vine leaf on the reverse. (Actual size approximately 25 mm.)

Second Revolt coins, the size of a quarter-shekel or denarius, were made with many different designs related to sacred implements, grapes, and branches. All were overstruck on old Roman coins. (Actual size approximately 19 mm.)

The overstriking was a means of converting offensive money into something more worthy of use by devout Jews. The new coins were also given new names: the denarius was called a *zuz*, and the tetradrachm, or shekel, equal to four Roman denarii, became a *sela*. The largest and most impressive of the Bar Kokhba coins is the silver *sela* (shekel) that shows the façade of the Temple of Jerusalem, with the Ark of the Covenant and scrolls displayed inside.

An illustration of life in Jerusalem during the Aelia Capitolina period.

After the revolt had been subdued by a massive legionary force in 134, the Romans proceeded to build their new city on the site of Jerusalem. They named it Aelia Capitolina and erected a temple to Jupiter. Thus, the hopes and dreams of the Jews to rebuild the Holy Temple of Jehovah were crushed, leaving behind a legacy of coins as a reminder of the glorious past.

THE BEGINNINGS OF CHRISTIANITY

It's important to bear in mind that "the Bible" is not a uniform book. Though the term often includes sacred texts of both Judaism and Christianity, throughout the years different religious groups have included different portions of these ancient texts, sometimes also placing them in different order. The Hebrew Bible, or *Tanakh*, contains 24 books, which include "teaching," "prophets," and "writings." The first part of the Christian Bible, called the Old Testament, contains much of the Hebrew Bible text, plus additional books. The second part, called the New Testament, is based on the teachings of Jesus of Nazareth and contains the letters and various writings of his apostles and early church figures. Different interpretations of what is known as the Christian Bible are in the Roman Catholic, Protestant, Ethiopian, and various Orthodox canons.

The Bible that Jesus knew was the Tanakh. The New Testament was written only after his Ascension, by his followers who still considered themselves to be Jewish. Theirs was a blending of beliefs in two religious convictions. The later transition from Judaism to Christianity was a slow and tedious passage. The apostles and disciples preached the word about him through their travels and writing. Their accounts of his miracles and deeds were eventually recorded and compiled in the form now known as the New Testament.

CONTINUING THE WORK OF THE LORD

Directly after the death of Jesus, his devoted apostles began their mission to spread his teachings to a vast audience. Their initial goal was not to formulate a new religion, but rather to shed fresh insight into past traditions and strengthen belief in salvation. Their task was confirmed by Jesus, as recorded in Matthew 28:16–19, "Therefore go and make disciples of all nations," as well as in Mark 16:15, "Go into all the world and preach the gospel to all creation."

Many who heard the apostles resisted any change from their traditional beliefs, while others felt the time was at hand for the promised messiah to appear and free them from the tyranny of their Roman captors. Also in the audience were people of various faiths, who listened with curiosity and interest to the words of this pious man whose messages, marvels, and good deeds were seen as prophetic and admirable. It was into this muddled mixture of political and religious turmoil that Christianity attempted to gain a foothold and expand beyond Jerusalem.

Aiding in the work of the apostles was a growing cadre of new believers who we know as disciples. In some accounts of their proselytizing efforts they are called either disciples or apostles, as the terms are somewhat interchangeable, but the word disciple is factually more accurate. The original 12 apostles are recorded in the Gospel of Matthew as: Simon (re-named Peter); Andrew; James; John (son of Zebedee); Philip; Bartholomew; Thomas; Matthew; James (son of Alphaeus); Thaddaeus; Simon; and Judas Iscariot.

Early converts to Christianity were probably all Jews living in Jerusalem and the towns and villages of Palestine, prior to the conversion of the Roman officer Cornelius (in Acts 10). Within the early church there was a distinction between Hellenistic and non-Hellenistic Jews, but with the acceptance of Cornelius a new group, called *Gentiles*, was recognized. This adaptation was the first of many debates over whether converts to the new church must first convert to Judaism and follow its regulations.

> *While talking with him, Peter went inside and found a large gathering of people. He said to them: "You are well aware that it is against our law for a Jew to associate with or visit a Gentile. But God has shown me that I should not call anyone impure or unclean. (Acts 10:27–28)*

One of the earliest converts was a Pharisee named Saul, who was later known as Paul. He had formerly been a fierce opponent of the new sect but was miraculously changed when he went to arrest believers in Damascus. His conversion happened at about the same time as Cornelius the centurion.

The conversion of Paul on the road to Damascus.

In Antioch, the capital of the province of Syria, many people became believers, and it was there that they were first called Christians. It was from Antioch that Paul and Barnabas traveled to Cyprus in about A.D. 46 to preach the Gospel. Paul's conversion of both Jews and Gentiles to the new faith sparked a controversy as to whether non-Jews could be accepted as Christians. In a conference held at Jerusalem in A.D. 49, decisions were made to welcome all converts and to curtail the involvement of non-Jews in keeping traditional Jewish rituals.

***Paul and Barnabas at Lystra,* Jacob Pynas (c. 1605–1650).**

As the new religion grew and solidified, efforts were made to spread the word of Christ as far as possible. Paul made missionary journeys into Europe, and by A.D. 64 there were churches in all the main centers of the Roman Empire. The city of Antioch became the major hub of the new Christian church. Efforts to establish and promote the new religion met with resistance from many quarters, but none more violent and abusive than from the emperors of Rome.

Herod Agrippa, the grandson of Herod the Great, was educated in Rome and was a friend of Caligula and Claudius. Strongly pro-Jewish, Agrippa persecuted the Christians, had James killed, and imprisoned Peter. The procurator Antonius Felix, who served under Claudius from A.D. 52 to 54 and under Nero A.D. 55 to 62, caused the apostle Paul to be sentenced to prison at Caesarea. Under Emperor Nero, in Rome, the situation was even worse: thousands of Christians were savagely killed for sport and entertainment, and the apostles Peter and Paul were martyred. The old legend that Nero "fiddled" while Rome burned is based on his dedication to the arts; he often dressed in the robes of Apollo and played the lyre or recited poetry. One of his copper coins, made near the time of the great fire of Rome in A.D. 64 (which he blamed on the Christians), shows him in such a performance.

Roman Emperor Claudius (A.D. 42–43), shown on the obverse of this bronze coin called an "as," with Minerva on the reverse, was an early persecutor of the Christians. (Actual size approximately 30 mm.)

The early Church suffered under the rule of Emperor Nero, who blamed the Christians for starting the fire that destroyed much of Rome in A.D. 64. He is shown on one of his coins playing the lyre. (Actual size approximately 30 mm.)

The Roman emperor Domitian's persecution of the Jews included a tax on all those who "lived a Jewish life" or "drifted into Jewish ways." At that time the Romans did not consider Christianity to be a separate religion from Judaism. Similarly, the early Christians probably considered themselves to be a sect within Judaism. After Domitian's death in A.D. 96 and the emergence of a more tolerant emperor, Nerva, the rules of tax collection were relaxed and limited to those who openly practiced Judaism. By this measure, the Christians escaped the tax, but they were not officially recognized as a separate religion until the Edict of Milan in 313.

In the Edict of Milan, Roman emperors Constantine and Licinius proclaimed, "It is proper that Christians and all others should have liberty to follow that mode of religion which to each of them appears

The Journeys of the Apostles

In addition to Paul's herculean efforts, the other apostles divided the world into territories and headed out in all directions—from Armenia to Ethiopia and from India to Spain, as well as traveling to Jewish communities around the Mediterranean Sea, attracting numerous converts, many of whom also spread the word.

Peter, also known as Simon Peter, was one of the twelve apostles and one of the first leaders of the early church. He was known to be outspoken, and one of the boldest witnesses of the new faith. He was born about 1 B.C. and died sometime around A.D. 67. According to Christian tradition, he was crucified in Rome under Emperor Nero.

A fresco from a church in Prague of the apostles Peter and John performing healing miracles.

The travels of Peter included areas around Pontus, Galatia, Cappadocia, Asia, and Bithynia (1 Peter 1:1), where he preached to "strangers," indicating they were Jewish immigrants. These were the lands that, according to the Jewish historian Josephus, were the dwelling place of the Ten Tribes. In *Antiquities of the Jews*, book XI, Chapter V.2, he states, "But then the entire body of the people of Israel remained in that country; wherefore there are but two tribes in Asia and Europe subject to the Romans, while the ten tribes are beyond Euphrates till now, and are an immense multitude."

Barnabas, who accompanied Paul on his trips, was an early Christian and one of the most prominent disciples in Jerusalem. According to Acts 4:36, he was a Cypriot Jew who undertook missionary work to defend Gentile converts against the Judaizers, a faction of Jewish Christians, both of Jewish and non-Jewish origins, who regarded the Levitical laws of the Old Testament as still binding on all Christians. They tried to enforce Jewish circumcision upon the Gentile converts to early Christianity, but Paul strenuously opposed and criticized their behavior, and he used many of his epistles to contest their efforts.

Andrew ministered to the Scythians and neighboring countries as his province. He also traveled to Nice, where he stayed for two years before moving on to Nicomedia, Heraclea, Amastris and Sinope. It was there that he met his brother, Peter, where he stayed for a time before returning to Jerusalem. Subsequently, Andrew also spread the gospel to the inhabitants of Cherson and Sinope.

Philip the Apostle was one of four disciples by that name who are often confused in various accounts of their activities. His mission was to Greece, Syria, Phrygia, and possibly also to Scythia. His journey ended around A.D. 58, at Caesarea, where he retired and raised his four daughters.

Matthias was born in Bethlehem of the Tribe of Judah, and he was selected by lot to replace Judas after the ascension of Jesus. He traveled on a three-year journey with the Apostle Andrew and was with him at Edessa and Sebaste. According to tradition, Matthias also preached in Pontine, Ethiopia, and Macedonia.

John may have been sent to Gaul, which is modern-day France. This is only based on a French legend that Mary, the mother of Jesus, went to Gaul, yet we know that the Messiah told John to take care of his mother. There is a legend that Mary went with John to France and later to Britain. Paul may have passed by Gaul on his way from Italy to Spain (Romans 15:24, 28), although there is no other historical proof that John went to Gaul.

Within ten years of the death of Jesus, the apostles and their many followers had attracted enthusiasts for this new way of life from Jerusalem to Antioch, Ephesus, Corinth, Thessalonica, Cyprus, Crete, Alexandria, and Rome. By the end of the first century, Christianity had spread throughout much of the Roman Empire despite strong opposition and persecution.

best." It thus granted tolerance to all religions, including Christianity, and went a step further than Emperor Galerius's edict of toleration in April 311, which had officially ended the Great Persecution.

Bronze portrait coins of Roman emperors Galerius and Licinius I.

Roman interference was not the only trial that early Christianity had to contend with as it spread. The Persian Empire, which had once tolerated Christianity, reversed its attitude upon the acceptance of that religion by their Roman rivals. A major persecution of Persian Christian churches was carried on between 340 and 363 after their wars had reopened upon Constantine's death. According to accounts, Shahpur II ordered the arrest of Simon, "chief of the Christians," and imposed a double tax and tribute on Persian Christians.

A silver drachma of Shahpur II, king of Persia, A.D. 309–379. The obverse shows a crowned and cuirassed bust facing right; on the reverse are a fire altar and attendants.

Despite many obstacles and the hardships imposed on the new religion, it continued to grow and flourish, in large part through the extensive travels and teachings of disciples Paul, Peter, Philip, Mark, and Barnabas. Collectors of what are commonly known as "coins of the Bible" frequently add examples of coins from each of the various locations where disciples visited and spread their faith. Many such coins are inexpensive treasures that provide a virtual trip through time and space.

THE JOURNEYS OF PAUL

It was into this mixture of political and religious turmoil that Christianity attempted to gain a foothold and expand to places beyond Jerusalem. The apostle Paul's journey in A.D. 46 took him and Barnabas from their base at Antioch in Syria by ship to Cyprus, and from there to present-day Turkey. His second journey in A.D. 48 to 51 included an 18-month stay in Corinth. All along the way, new churches were established, and his teachings were recorded in writings that have come down to us as New Testament text. The cities that he visited can be traced through contemporary coins in a way that captures the imagination of many collectors.

> *And one night the Lord said to Paul in a vision, "Do not fear, but speak and do not keep silence; because I am with thee, and no one shall attack thee or injure thee, for I have many people in this city." So he settled there a year and six months teaching the word of God among them.* (Acts 18:10–11)

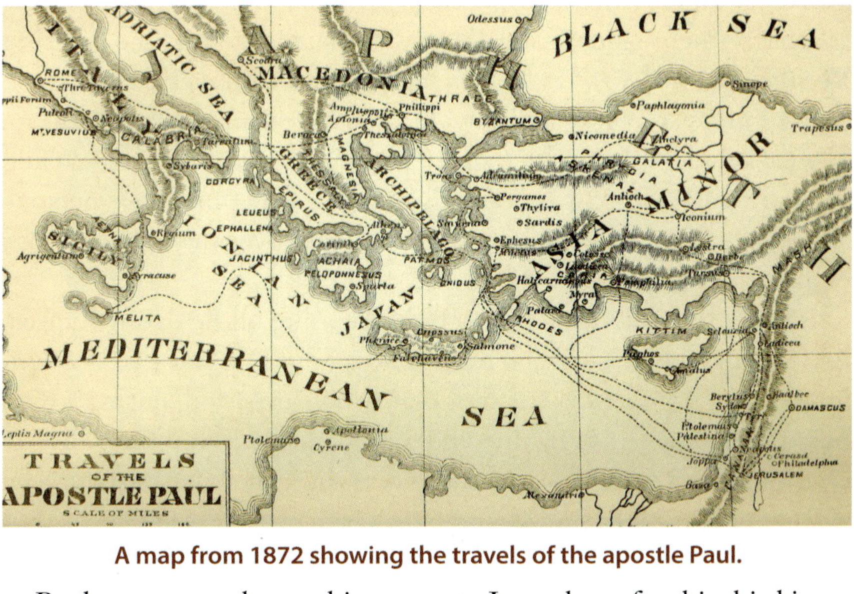

A map from 1872 showing the travels of the apostle Paul.

Paul was arrested upon his return to Jerusalem after his third journey. He spent the next two years (A.D. 58–60) in prison, before appealing to be heard by the emperor. Luke accompanied him when he set sail for Rome, but this time he was under guard and his missionary activities were curtailed. In Rome, Christians came out to meet him, and for the next two years Paul continued to preach the message of Jesus, though under house arrest and awaiting trial.

Bronze coin of Caesarea, 228 A.D. Coins of Ephesus, Phoenicia, Caesarea, and Antioch would have been familiar to early Christians in places where Paul traveled to spread the word of the Gospel. "When the brothers learned of this, they brought him down to Caesarea and sent him forth to Tarsus" (Acts 9:30).

Paul's extensive missionary work included areas around the Aegean Sea such as Miletus, Ephesus, Neapolis, Philippi, Berea, Thessalonica, Athens, and Corinth. He also apparently used the amazing Roman road network (as well as sea voyages) to travel across Israel, Syria, Turkey, Greece, and Italy. It has been calculated that to do so, he may have traveled more than 10,000 miles, mostly by foot! While an admirable record, it is certainly very possible, for I have personally equaled that in my daily exercising walks over the same number of years.

It was Paul's intention to teach the Gentiles, as he did in Cyprus, Asia Minor, and Greece. To his detriment, his brashness landed him in prison in Rome. At the end of that two-year period, during which no accusers appeared, Paul would automatically have been released according to Roman law. At that point, he concluded his work by visiting the Lost Ten Tribes and ministering in southern Galatia, but he was not allowed to minister in other areas, as stated in Matthew 10:5-6: "Go not into the way of the Gentiles, and into any city of the Samaritans enter ye not: but go rather to the lost sheep of the house of Israel."

Christian martyrs in the Roman Colosseum.

By the end of the first century, Christianity had spread throughout much of the Roman Empire despite strong opposition and persecution. Several of the Roman emperors who followed Nero were tolerant of the new religion, as long as it did not interfere with their personal preference or the numerous deities that were sacred to the Romans. One notable exception was Elagabalus (218–222), who was the hereditary priest of the Syrian sun god Heliogabalus. The excesses of this depraved emperor (who was assassinated at the age of 18) were somewhat mitigated during the reign of Philip I (244–249), who some believe was the first Roman emperor to adopt Christianity as a personal religion. It is known that his wife, Otacilia Severa, was devoted to Christianity and made pilgrimages to Antioch at the time of Easter. Coins of these historical figures are relatively common and can be easily acquired by collectors.

Emperor Philip I and his wife Otacilia Severa (A.D. 244–249) were possibly the first Roman rulers to adopt the new Christian religion. Otacilia is known to have been a true believer and devoted member of the church of Antioch. (Top pair, actual size approximately 25 mm. Bottom pair, actual size approximately 24 mm.)

Elagabalus issued this bronze coin at Antioch in A.D. 218–222 for use in the Roman colonies. It has the portrait of this young man who was devoted to the sun god and tried to impose his religion on the entire empire. (Actual size approximately 25 mm.)

Elagabalus's grandmother, Julia Maesa, was far more tolerant of other religions and curtailed Christian persecution. (Actual size approximately 19 mm.)

Emperor Diocletian issued this bronze coin about the same time that he was issuing many harsh decrees against the Christians. (Actual size approximately 29 mm.)

The last great Roman persecutor of Christians was Emperor Diocletian (A.D. 285–305). One irony of his reign is that despite his cruelty, one of his reforms—the division of the Roman Empire into districts called dioceses—continues to be employed in the organization of the Roman Catholic Church, the Anglican Communion, and other churches to the present day.

ROME ACCEPTS CHRISTIANITY

The first Roman emperor to recognize Christianity as a religion was Constantine I, the Great (A.D. 307–337). It is said that in a military campaign in what is now Italy, Constantine beheld in the heavens a flaming cross bearing the inscription *In hoc signo vinces* ("By this sign you will conquer"). The following night, the cross again appeared to him in a dream, and he was told to use this sign as his emblem. The decisive battle at the Milvian Bridge in A.D. 312 was then successful and motivated his edict that embraced the new religion. From that time forward, the Roman sun god was removed from Constantine's coins and replaced with non-religious depictions.

Constantine's vision and the Battle of the Milvian Bridge.

Constantine is reputed to have been baptized and converted to Christianity on his deathbed. Prior to that, he led a life that was anything but religious (including the murder of his wife and son), and was more devoted to the Roman sun god Sol. About two years before he died, he established Sunday as the day of worship. He also moved the capital of the empire from Rome to Byzantium, naming the new city Constantinople. Despite his mixed religious behaviors, Constantine was strongly influenced throughout his life by his mother Helena, a devout Christian who is believed to have discovered the remains of the true cross upon which Jesus was crucified.

A fourteenth-century icon depicting Constantine I and Helena.

Constantine intervened in ecclesiastical affairs to achieve unity; he presided over the first ecumenical council of the church at Nicaea in 325, and he built churches in the Holy Land, where his mother is credited with identifying numerous places associated with biblical events. Coins with Helena's portrait

Facts & Folklore

Fourth-Century Discoverer of Holy Relics

Saint Helena was converted to Christianity late in life. She was the mother of Constantine the Great and used her high position and wealth in the service of her adopted religion. She helped build churches throughout the empire, and nearing age 80 she led a goodwill tour of the Holy Land where she reputedly discovered the True Cross and other religious artifacts (see pages 172–173). Her portrait can be seen on Roman coins made periodically by her son Emperor Constantine I (c. A.D. 318 to 329) and her three grandsons during and shortly after her lifetime.

Helena, mother of Constantine the Great, was converted to Christianity and made pilgrimages to the Holy Land where she reputedly discovered many holy relics. Her image can be seen on Roman bronze coins minted c. A.D. 326. (Actual size approximately 19 mm.)

were minted by her son, but none of them show any of the religious scenes connected to her discoveries.

With the favorable conditions established by Constantine, the Christian religion grew and flourished not only in Rome but throughout the Mediterranean. Various symbols like the flaming cross adopted by Constantine slowly began to appear on coins, in place of the pagan gods that had preceded them. The most prominent of these was the familiar XP symbol known as the Christogram, or Chi-Rho monogram. The Greek letters are an abbreviation for the name Jesus Christ and are believed to have been the emblem seen by Constantine in his vision.

In the early years of Constantine's reign, some designs used on his coins included a dedication to the sun god Sol. The one shown above depicts the radiant Sol Invicto standing and holding a globe. After Constantine's victorious battle at the Milvian Bridge, some of his coins show a Christogram (XP) that became his personal religious badge. (Actual size approximately 17 mm.)

Emperor Theodosius I (379–395) issued the first Roman coins to include a distinct Christian cross. From those first bronze pieces, the cross was used in increasing prominence on many issues of the Byzantine Empire. A fish was occasionally used as an early Christian symbol, but it does not seem to have ever appeared on any coin.

Coin of Emperor Theodosius.

This bronze double centenionalis, issued in A.D. 350 by Emperor Magnentius, was the first coin with a design devoted exclusively to Christianity. Although an avowed Christian, Magnentius also restored certain rights to the pagans. (Actual size approximately 27 mm.)

The last Roman emperor to strenuously resist the new religion was Julian II, A.D. 360–363, who wanted to restore polytheism. His large bronze coins depict a cult bull. (Actual size approximately 26 mm.)

A Roman bronze coin of Julian II with youthful portrait.

For many years the XP symbol was used as part of the design on numerous coins of the Roman and Byzantine empires. When Magnentius became emperor in A.D. 350, he used the monogram as the principal design on some of his coins, even though he was not a true Christian. From then on, the only Roman emperor to shun the Christian religion was Julian II, the Apostate, who for a short period from 360 to 363 attempted to restore the old pagan Roman religions.

In 363 Emperor Jovian (363–364) reinstituted anti-pagan laws that had been abolished by Julian II during his reign. When Julian was killed in battle with the Sassanid Persians, Jovian was hastily declared emperor by his soldiers. He sought peace with the Persians on terms that cost the Romans a significant amount of territory; however, he did restore Christianity to the empire as the favored religion.

THE CONVERSION OF AXUM

In the early part of the fourth century after the birth of Jesus, three major nations adopted some form of participation in a new religious experience. The first of these was the open acceptance of Christianity in Rome. Almost immediately thereafter, the fresh new faith spread throughout Axum (Ethiopia) and Armenia, where it became the state religion.

For many years the Axumite kingdom held a favorable and prosperous position as a marine trading center, with commercial ties to Arabia, Egypt, India, and Rome by the second century A.D. It soon began minting its own coins, the first of which depicted a bust of the king along with pagan symbols of the sun and moon.

The kingdom reached the height of its success under King Ezana, who reigned from about 325 to 370. It was during this time that the king was converted to Christianity and established it as the dominant religion. Under him, Frumentius was consecrated as the first Bishop of Axum by the Coptic Church of Alexandria. Shortly thereafter, Ezana replaced the symbols on his coins with Coptic crosses. Axum was the first African state to adopt Christianity, and while that still remains the majority religion today, modern-day Ethiopia is also home to many Muslim and Jewish citizens.

Gold 1/3 solidus of Ezana. Note the cross above the king's head.

Tradition holds that Menelik I, who became the first emperor of Ethiopia sometime around 950 B.C., was the son of the Queen of Sheba and King Solomon. Menelik is credited with bringing the Biblical Ark of the Covenant to Ethiopia. The Ethiopian Orthodox Church claims that the Church of Our Lady Mary of Zion in Aksum still houses the Ark, in which lie the Tablets of Law upon which the Ten Commandments are inscribed.

The Ark of the Covenant arrives in Axum (Ethiopia) with Menelik I.

THE CONVERSION OF ARMENIA

Armenia's conversion to Christianity was not without its share of obstacles. There were converts in the area as early as the first century through the missionary efforts of Thaddaeus, Bartholomew, and Jude. The greatest evangelist was Saint Gregory the Parthian. After the Persians overtook the country in 238 to 250, governance of Armenia was given to King Tridates III, who considered Christians to be disturbers of the peace. When the king fell ill, he had Gregory brought to him in hopes of a cure. Moved by his miraculous recovery, Tridates accepted Christianity, along with his entire court.

The king helped Gregory to build the city of Etchmiadzin (called "the place where the Only Son descended"), which in time became the holy center of the Armenian Catholics. Having finished his work, he entrusted the patriarchate to his son Aristaces, who attended the famous Coun-

A mosaic of St. Gregory in the Pammakaristos Church in Istanbul.

cil of Nicaea in 325, when the faith was adopted as the national Armenian religion. The church, whose dogma at first was that of Rome and Byzantium, separated from them in 491 because of its refusal to acknowledge the trinity of Christ. Afterward, the newly separate church became known as the Gregorian Church, in honor of its founder.

Bronze *kardez* of Armenia's Christian king Gosdantin I, 1298–1299.

THE BYZANTINE EMPIRE

Constantinople became a capital of the Roman Empire in 330 when Constantine the Great renamed the city of Byzantium after himself. It gradually developed into the true capital of the eastern Roman provinces, which included southeastern Europe and parts of southwestern Asia. Also embraced were the northeast corner of Africa, the present-day countries of the Balkan Peninsula, as well as Syria, Jordan, Israel, Lebanon, and Cyprus.

The Byzantine Empire ran from the reign of Anastasius I (491–518) to the capture of Constantinople by the Turks in 1453. The Seljuk Turks, after making devastating raids into Byzantium's eastern territories, crushed an imperial army at the Battle of Manzikert (1071) and overran most of Byzantine Asia Minor. Meanwhile, the Byzantines lost their last foothold in Italy and were alienated from the Christian West by a schism (1054) between the Orthodox Church and the Papacy. Alongside this period of political upheaval, Christian practices and values also developed significantly.

The most interesting Byzantine coins of this period are those with portraits of Jesus and his mother Mary. Despite being some of the most ancient of all images of the Holy Family, none of these portraits

A sixth-century mosaic showing Mary and young Jesus.

pre-dates the year 685, and all are probably imaginative representations. The standardized bust of Christ most often used is, however, the one that was widely accepted, and it has continued to be used as a standard representation of Jesus in art ever since.

Few earlier images of Christ exist. The most ancient is a late third-century fresco from the cemetery of Saints Peter and Marcellinus in Rome, showing Christ with light skin, short hair, and a clean-shaven face. There is also a fourth-century sarcophagus from Rome that likewise shows him with short hair and clean-shaven. A fifth-century ivory plaque from Sicily (now in the Victoria and Albert Museum) shows the adult Christ as clean-shaven, but with long hair.

The earliest depiction of Christ in the "traditional" style used on most Byzantine coins is found on a sixth-century painted icon that depicts the nimbate (with halo) bust of Christ facing, dispensing a blessing and holding a book of gospels. He is bearded and has long, wavy hair and rather slender features. The image is strikingly similar to that used on a gold solidus of Byzantine Emperor Justinian II, made during his first reign (A.D. 685–695). In that depiction, a cross set behind the head replaces the nimbus, but the similarity is unmistakable.

The first coined image of Christ appeared on gold pieces of the Byzantine Emperor Justinian II, A.D. 685–695. On the earliest coins he is shown with traditional long hair and beard. A second version of the portrait is seen on later gold solidi, made in A.D. 705–711, with curly hair and no beard. (Actual size approximately 22 mm.)

Byzantine bronze coins in the first millennium A.D. often showed images of Christ or the Virgin Mary. (Actual size approximately 26 mm.)

During the second reign of Justinian (705–711), a different image of Christ is used. This one, for which there is still no explanation, depicts a shaven man with short, curly hair. Use of the Christ image was short-lived at this time because of the impending iconoclastic movement, which sought to suppress all religious images. At the Seventh Ecumenical Council of Constantinople in A.D. 754, the Church declared that such representations would no longer be tolerated:

> *Supported by the Holy Scriptures and the Fathers, we declare unanimously, in the name of the Holy Trinity, that there shall be rejected and removed and cursed out of the Christian Church every likeness which is made out of any material and color whatever by the evil art of painters.*

With the death of Emperor Theophilus in 842, the iconoclast controversy ended, and Michael III reinstated the Christ-image on his gold coins. Christian images would appear on the vast majority of Byzantine coins until the end of the Empire. Most Byzantine copper coins tend to suffer from years of circulation, repetitive designs, poor minting techniques, and inferior artistry. Yet these coins are significant for their vibrant iconography, and deserve to be studied for their historical aspects as well as their Christian imagery.

Many ancient depictions of Jesus, and perhaps other biblical figures, were destroyed and forever lost before the General Council of approximately 350 bishops at Nicaea reversed the unfortunate decree in A.D. 787. The coins of Justinian II are among the few remaining early images of Christ, and the only icons generally available for public appreciation outside of museums. His gold coins are scarce and valuable, but fortunately for collectors, the imagery was revised in later years and used on many gold and bronze coins that are regularly available.

A nimbate illustration of Jesus from 1183.

Recovery of the True Cross

Byzantine emperor Heraclius (610–641) played an important part in promulgating the Christian religion through his participation in recovering an ancient artifact known as the True Cross during his war against the Persians. This important relic was reputed to be the very wood upon which Christ was crucified. Historians assume this event took place near the years 626 to 628. A bronze follis coin of Heraclius shows the emperor displaying the holy relic as he stands in triumph with his son.

Heraclius battles Khosrow II.

A bronze follis (30 mm.) showing Heraclius, holding a long cross, and Heraclius Constantine, holding a globus cruciger, with a cross above; c. A.D. 629–631.

A coin of Khosrow II.

According to popular belief, the emperor was involved in a battle against the Sassanid king Khosrow II (591–628), who had stolen the cross when he sacked Jerusalem in 614. Heraclius decisively defeated the Sassanid Persians at the Battle of Nineveh and recovered the cross. The artifact was taken back to Jerusalem amid great rejoicing, and together with Patriarch Zacharios (609–632) Heraclius placed it in the Temple of the Resurrection for veneration. In 1009 Jerusalem was attacked by the Fatimid caliph al-Hakim (996–1021) and the church was destroyed. What became of the artifact after that remains a matter of faith and tradition. The cross was purported to have originally been discovered by Saint Helena during construction of the Church of the Holy Sepulcher in Jerusalem, during the reign of her son, Emperor Constantine I (see pages 161–163).

The discovery of the True Cross.

IMAGES OF JESUS

If you had walked down the streets of Judaea during the lifetime of Jesus, would you have recognized him? Probably not, for he undoubtedly looked very much like the other inhabitant of that time and place.

There were no contemporary drawings, images, or written descriptions to aid in identification. Sadly, we are still without that kind of detailed information about his appearance.

Jesus likely has been written about, talked about, and thought about more than any other person in history. Despite that, very little is known about his precise appearance. Contemporary anthropologists have attempted to simulate his facial features based on genetic background evidence, but to little avail. The New Testament books of apostles Matthew and Luke give two different accounts of his genealogy, tracing it back to the time of King David. Thus, we are left to ponder the appearance of Jesus based mostly on scant available genetic evidence.

Most first-century Palestinian Jews could have been descended from David, and very likely many were. Jesus lived in Galilee nearly all his life and possibly spoke with a regional accent, like his neighbors. Matthew 1:16 indicates that Jesus was descended from King David through the line of David's son Solomon, tracing the lineage back to Abraham. Luke 3:23–38 traces the genealogy from Jesus to Adam. His mother, Mary, was also descended along similar lines and contributed to his genetic makeup. Yet, even these clues fail to give us a comprehensive glimpse of his appearance.

A brief account of the development of some early portraiture of Jesus is given on pages 168–170, expanding on a third-century portrait that shows a man with light skin, short hair, and a clean-shaven face. It also discusses the Byzantine portraiture from the sixth century and the development of the Pantocrator image, the basis of many of the representations seen ever since.

Conceivably, this dearth of knowledge about the actual countenance of Jesus was intentionally ordained, so that forever after everyone could envision him as we see ourselves, regardless of race, creed, or color.

A journey into better understanding and appreciating the Holy Bible is reinforced by the abundant existence of solid evidence, such as contemporary coins, pottery, and other artifacts, that remain with us to be studied, seen, touched, and examined by all.

When Jesus spoke again to the people, he said, "I am the light of the world. Whoever follows me will never walk in darkness, but will have the light of life." (John 8:12)

The Mesha Stele.

Appendix A

Digging into the Past

The earliest published document related to Old Testament history is a copy of a stone stele that was discovered in Jerusalem in 1868 and subsequently preserved in the Louvre. Unfortunately, the original has long been broken and sold as pieces.

The text is written in Moabite, dated to the ninth century B.C., and begins: "I am Mesha son of Chemosh, king of Moab." Included in the text is the king's account of a war fought with Israel in 850 B.C., in which Moab revolted against King Jehoram of the northern kingdom of Israel after the death of Ahab. This same event is mentioned in 2 Kings 3.

In 1872, George Smith claimed that he had discovered an account of a great flood described on Assyrian tablets that came from excavations of seventh century B.C. Nineveh, which were stored in the British Museum. The full story was recorded on 12 clay tablets and is called "The Epic of Gilgamesh." In it, the god Ea warned of a coming flood and told a man named Utnapishtim to build a boat called the *Preserver of Life*.

The full story is nearly identical to the biblical narrative of Noah in Genesis 6–9, including sending birds out from the boat to find out if the flood had receded. However, Utnapishtim's ark included not only his family and animals, but also people from his village.

A number of other clay tablets with cuneiform writing related to Canaanite history have been found in excavations since 1929. More than 1,500 have been published detailing events from the fifteenth to thirteenth centuries B.C., giving insight into parallels between Canaanite and Israelite religions.

Perhaps the most important archeological discovery confirming the accuracy of biblical accounts was the 1947 finding of over 800 fragments of documents in a cave on the western side of the Dead Sea. The trove included Hebrew writings on parchment and leather relating to 190 biblical scrolls, including a complete Isaiah scroll, and other Old Testament references dating from the mid-third century to the first or second century B.C.

Equally significant is the discovery of a stone cave burial site at Ketef Hinnom, near Jerusalem, that was made in 1979 by Israeli archaeologist Gabriel Barkay. The find was only partially published until translations were completed in 1989. Among the items found in the burial ossuary were two small silver scrolls. Due to their fragile nature, it took technicians three years to unroll them so that they could be read.

One of the copper scrolls found among the Dead Sea Scrolls at Qumran.

One of the first words to be deciphered was the name "Yahwea"; eventually, the scrolls were dated to the late seventh century B.C. They contain the Benediction from Numbers 6:24–26, a short and beautiful prayer known as Aaron's Blessing that is set in poetic form and is one of the oldest poems in the Bible.

In 1993, excavators at Tel Dan, Israel, uncovered an inscription with words that referred to the "House of David," dated to the ninth century B.C. The Aramaic writing on the stele

The Ketef Hinnom cave.

also mentions victory over the Israelite King Jehoram, son of Ahab, a figure who also appears in the biblical book of 2 Kings. While the precise meaning of the reference to the House of David is uncertain, most scholars agree it pertains to the biblical King David, a very important part of Israel's history.

Certainly, future excavations and discoveries will disclose additional information about the events and people recorded in Old and New Testament accounts, corroborating the dedicated work of archaeologists and research workers and bringing a fuller understanding of these ancient epochs.

The Tel Dan Stele.

The view from within the fortifications at Masada.

Appendix B

Additional Reading

The Antiquities of the Jews. Flavius Josephus. Translated by William Whiston. Various editions. Since 93 A.D.

Numismatic Illustrations of the Narrative Portions of the New Testament. John Yonge Akerman. London, 1846.

History of Jewish Coinage, and of Money in the Old and New Testament. Frederic W. Madden. Quaritch, 1864.

Jewish Coins. Théodore Reinach. 1903. Reprinted in 1966.

Early Christian Numismatics and Other Antiquarian Tracts. C.W. King. London, 1873.

Christian Teaching of Coin Mottoes. Wm. Allan and J. Zimmerman. London, 1911.

A Handy Guide to Jewish Coins. Rev. J.E. Rogers. London, 1914.

They Wrote on Clay: The Babylonian Tablets Speak Today. Howard Chiera. Chicago, 1938.

Shekel Medals and False Shekels. Bruno Kisch. Reprinted from Historia Judaica. New York, 1941.

Ancient Coins Associated with Christianity. Charles Tuckwood. Reprinted from *The Numismatist*. ANA, 1947.

Ancient Jewish Coins. A. Reifenberg. Jerusalem, 1947, 1973.

Money Talks About the Bible. G.R. Halliday, 1948.

Ancient Hebrew Arts. A. Reifenberg. New York, 1950.

The Dating of the Shekel. J.U. Gillespie. Reprinted from *The Numismatist*. ANA, 1950.

Israel's History in Coins. A. Reifenberg. London, 1953.

Coins of Bible Days. Florence Aiken Banks. New York, 1955.

The Dating and Meaning of Ancient Jewish Coins and Symbols. Israel Numismatic Society. Jerusalem, 1958.

Israel's Money. Leo Kadman. Israel Numismatic Society. Jerusalem, 1959.

The Numismatic Iconography of Justinian II. James D. Breckenridge. ANS New York, 1959.

The Day Christ Was Born. Jim Bishop. New York, 1959, 1960.

Moneys of the Bible. R.S. Yeoman. Whitman Publishing. Racine, WI, 1961.

Archaeology and the Types of Greek Coins. Percy Gardner. Chicago, 1965.

Star in the East. Hans Holzer. New York, 1968.
The Pleasures of Archaeology. Karl E. Meyer. New York, 1971.
Bar-Kokhba: The Rediscovery of the Legendary Hero of the Second Jewish Revolt Against Rome. Yigael Yadin. Tel Aviv, 1971.
Jewish Symbols on Ancient Jewish Coins. Paul Romanoff. New York, 1971.
Coins and the Bible. Martin Price. London, 1975.
The Ancient World. Early Writing from Mesopotamia and Egypt. Kenneth Rendell. Newton, MA, 1979.
Coins and Christianity. Kenneth Jacob. London, 1959, 1985.
Biblical Related Coins. James B. Lovett. Little Rock, AR, 1985, 1986.
Coins of the Jewish-Roman Wars. H. Kogen. Israel, 1987.
Guide to Biblical Coins. David Hendin. New York, 1987–2010, 2022.
Official Guide to Artifacts of Ancient Civilizations. Alex G Malloy. New York, 1997.
Nelson's Illustrated Encyclopedia of the Bible. Edited by John Drane. Oxford, 1998.
The Numismatic Legacy of the Jews. Samuels, Rynearson, Meshorer. New York, 2000.
Biblical Numismatics: Thirty Pieces of Silver. Shirley Barr Sage. Arizona, 2001.
Coins of the Bible. Arthur L. Friedberg. Whitman Publishing, Atlanta, GA, 2004.
Money of the Bible. Kenneth Bressett. Whitman Publishing, Atlanta, GA, 2005, 2006, 2013.
Milestone Coins. Kenneth Bressett. Whitman Publishing, Atlanta, GA, 2007.
A Numismatic Journey Through the Bible. Richard J. Plant. Trafalgar Square, 2007.
Cultural Change: Jewish, Christian, and Islamic Coins of the Holy Land. David Hendin. New York 2011.
Ancient Coins Through the Bible. Joseph A. Dow. Tate Publishing, 2011.
Coins of the Holy Land. Volumes 1 and 2. Meshorer and Bijovsky. ANS and Israel Museum. New York, 2012.
Coins and the Bible. Richard Abdy and Amelia Dowler. British Museum. London, 2013.
Dated Coins of Antiquity. Edward E. Cohen. Classical Numismatic Group, Lancaster, PA, 2014.
Jesus and the Jewish Roots of Mary. Brant Pitre. New York, 2018.
"Atlas of the Bible: Exploring the Holy Lands." Jean-Pierre Isbouts. National Geographic, 2018.
The Handbook of Biblical Numismatics. Mel Wacks. Israel Numismatic Service, Houston, 1976. www.amuseum.org/book.
The Handbook of Biblical Numismatics. 45th Anniversary edition. Mel Wacks. 2021. https://nnp.wustl.edu/library/book/600117

Appendix C

A Gallery of Biblical Coins

The following coin images are shown at their actual size and in chronological order, to allow the reader to better visualize these coins in daily use thousands of years ago.

Ancient electrum pre-coin money units.

Silver half stater of Lydia, 561–546 B.C.

Silver staters of Aegina, c. 525 B.C.

Athenian tetradrachm, c. 500–400 B.C.

Macedonian silver tetradrachm of Mende, c. 500–400 B.C.

Silver stater of Corinth.

Sidon double shekel, c. 400–300 B.C.

Silver Judaean coin, c. 375 to 333 B.C.

Silver shekel of Byblos, c. 375–351 B.C.

Stater of Philip II, c. 359–336 B.C.

Silver tetradrachm of Macedon, c. 336–323 B.C.

Gold stater of Macedon, c. 336–323 B.C.

Silver stater of Pamphylia, c. 330–250 B.C.

Silver drachma of Macedon, c. 325 B.C.

Silver tetradrachm of Ptolemy I of Egypt, c. 323 B.C.

Silver tetradrachm of Seleucus I of Babylon, c. 312–281 B.C.

Silver tetradrachm of Ptolemy III, c. 230 B.C.

Silver tetradrachm of Rhodes, c. 229–205 B.C.

Roman didrachma, c. 225–215 B.C.

A silver tetradrachm of Antiochus III of Syria, c. 222–187 B.C.

A silver tetradrachm of Antiochus IV of Syria, c. 175–164 B.C.

Silver drachma of Aradus, c. 161 B.C.

Silver tetradrachm of Roman Macedon, c. 148–147 B.C.

Silver tetradrachm of Antiochus VII of Syria, c. 138–129 B.C.

Syrian copper minted for Jerusalem under Antiochus VII, c. 138–129 B.C.

Bronze prutah of John Hyrcanus I of Judaea, c. 130–104 B.C.

Phoenician didrachma of Tyre, c. 126 B.C.–A.D. 65.

Bronze prutah of Judah Aristobulus I of Judaea, c. 104–103 B.C.

Bronze lepton of Alexander Jannaeus of Judaea, c. 103–76 B.C.

Bronze assarion of Chios, c. 100–0 B.C.

Tetradrachm of Tigranes II of Armenia, c. 95–55 B.C.

Silver tetradrachm of Aradus, c. 80 B.C.

Bronze prutah of John Hyrcanus II of Judaea, c. 63 to 40 B.C.

Roman denarius of M. Aemilius Scaurus, c. 58 B.C.

Roman silver tetradrachm of Aulus Gabinius, c. 57–55 B.C.

Roman denarius of Aulus Plautius, c. 54 B.C.

Bronze prutah of Mattathias Antigonus of Judaea, c. 40–37 B.C.

Judaean eight-prutot coin of Herod I, c. 40–4 B.C.

Bronze two-prutot coin of Herod I, c. 40–4 B.C.

Bronze prutah of Herod I, c. 40–4 B.C.

Roman silver denarius, c. 15 B.C.

Bronze prutah of Aretas IV of Nabataea, c. 9 B.C.–A.D. 40.

Bronze coin of Antioch, c. 5–4 B.C.

Silver tetradrachm of Antioch, c. 4–3 B.C.

Judaean bronze prutah of Herod Archelaus, c. 4 B.C.–A.D. 6.

Coin of Herod Philip I, c. 4 B.C.–A.D. 34.

Judaean bronze coin of Herod Antipas, c. 4 B.C.–A.D. 39.

Judaean prutah of Coponius, c. A.D. 6–9.

Judaean prutah of Marcus Ambibulus, c. A.D. 9–12.

Tetradrachm of Tyre, c. A.D. 10.

Copper coin of Syria, Seleucia and Pieria, c. A.D. 12.

Roman denarius of Tiberius, c. A.D. 14–37.

Roman gold aureus of Tiberius, c. A.D. 14–37.

Judaean prutah of Valerius Gratus, c. A.D. 15–26.

Copper coin of Indo-Parthian King Gondophares, c. A.D. 20–60.

Roman silver tetradrachm of Alexandria, c. A.D. 21.

Prutah of Pontius Pilate, c. A.D. 29–31.

Bronze lepton of Pontius Pilate, c. A.D. 30.

Judaean prutah of Herod Agrippa, c. A.D. 37–44.

Roman as coin of Claudius, c. A.D. 42–43.

Coin of Herod Agrippa II, c. A.D. 48–98.

Judaean prutah of Antonius Felix, c. A.D. 52–62.

Roman coin of Nero, c. A.D. 54–68.

Bronze prutah of Porcius Festus, c. A.D. 59.

Roman tetradrachm of Antioch and neighboring districts, c. A.D. 64.

Judaean bronze coin, c. A.D. 65.

Coin of Armenia Minor, c. A.D. 66–67.

Judaean shekel, c. A.D. 66–70.

Roman bronze coin, c. A.D. 66–73.

Roman coin of Vespasian, c. A.D. 70–79.

Syrian bronze coin of Trajan, c. A.D. 114–115.

Shekel, or sela, of Simon Bar Kokhba, c. A.D. 132–135.

Roman silver denarius of Hadrian, c. A.D. 132.

Antioch bronze coin of Elagabalus, c. A.D. 218–222.

Roman coin of Philip I, c. A.D. 244–249.

Bronze coin of Caesarea, c. 228 A.D.

Roman bronze coin of Diocletian, c. A.D. 285–305.

Roman bronze coin of Galerius, c. A.D. 305–311.

Roman coin of Constantine, c. A.D. 306–337.

Roman bronze coin of Licinius I, c. A.D. 308–324.

Persian silver drachma of Shahpur II, c. A.D. 309–379.

Gold 1/3 solidus of Ezana of Axum, c. A.D. 320–360.

Roman bronze coin, c. A.D. 326.

Bronze double centenionalis of Magnentius, c. A.D. 350.

Roman bronze coin of Julian II, c. A.D. 360–363.

Roman coin of Theodosius, c. A.D. 379–395.

Coin of Khosrow II, c. A.D. 590–628.

Byzantine bronze follis, c. A.D. 629–631.

Byzantine coin of Justinian II, c. A.D. 685–695.

Byzantine coin of Justinian II, c. A.D. 705–711.

About the Author

Kenneth Bressett has been involved in the numismatic hobby since the 1940s. He has written many articles and is author or editor of more than two dozen related books on such diverse areas as ancient coins, paper money, English, and American coins. He is a past governor, vice president, and president of the American Numismatic Association, and a highly accomplished teacher and researcher.

He has served for many years as the editor, senior editor, and now editor emeritus of *A Guide Book of United States Coins*—at more than 25 million copies, one of the best-selling nonfiction titles in American publishing. As a former consultant to the U.S. Mint, Ken was instrumental in helping to implement the 50 State Quarters Program and in selecting many of the coins' reverse designs.

His autobiography, along with a history of Whitman Publishing and a biography of R.S. Yeoman, is recounted in *A Penny Saved: R.S. Yeoman and His Remarkable Red Book* (2021).

Ken is a founder of the Rittenhouse Society, a past appointee to the U.S. Assay Commission, and a past member of the Citizens Commemorative Coin Advisory Committee. He has been honored with the Numismatic Literary Guild's Clemy Award, the American Numismatic Society's Distinguished Service Award, the American Numismatic Association Medal of Merit, the ANA Farran Zerbe Memorial award, and induction into the Numismatic Hall of Fame (at ANA Headquarters in Colorado Springs). He is the namesake of the Kenneth E. Bressett Young Numismatist Literary Award, administered by the ANA and Whitman Publishing.

Acknowledgements

The author would like to thank Philip Bressett and Mary Sauder for their photography assistance; Jeff Garrett, Mike Gasvoda, and Travis Markel for contributing images; David Hendin for writing the foreword and contributing images; the Diocese of Colorado Springs for their review and imprimatur approval for this book; and the Whitman Publishing staff.

Image Credits

Most of the images in this book are from the Whitman Archives or the personal collection of Ken Bressett. The remaining images are credited below, by page number. Where multiple illustrations are found on a given page, they are credited by location, starting with number 1 at upper left and reading left to right, top to bottom.

Introduction: Page xiv, Bakusova / Shutterstock. Page xvii, Alan Roche / American Numismatic Society.

Chapter 1: Page xviii, public domain / Wikimedia Commons. Page 4, Philadelphia Museum of Art / Wikimedia Commons. Page 5, District Court for the Eastern District of New York / Wikimedia Commons. Page 8, Norman B. Leventhal Map Center / Wikimedia Commons.

Chapter 2: Page 13, David Hendin. Page 15, Simone Migliaro / Shutterstock. Page 16.1, Glowonconcept / Shutterstock. Page 20, John Theodor / Shutterstock. Page 21.1, Osama Shukir Muhammed Amin FRCP / Wikimedia Commons. Page 23, StockStudio Aerials / Shutterstock. Page 25, Marzolino / Shutterstock.

Chapter 3: Page 26, Massachusetts Bible Society / Wikimedia Commons. Page 28, Massachusetts Bible Society / Wikimedia Commons. Page 35, Jeff Garrett. Page 43.1, Classical Numismatic Group. Page 43.3, Capitoline Museums / Wikimedia Commons. Page 44.2, Museo del Prado / Wikimedia Commons. Page 50, public domain / Wikimedia Commons.

Chapter 4: Page 58, ruskpp / Shutterstock. Page 61, Brooklyn Museum / Wikimedia Commons. Page 66, Musée d'Orsay. Page 68, public domain / Wikimedia Commons.

Chapter 5: Page 70, David Hendin. Page 76.1, Zde / Wikimedia Commons. Page 78, David Hendin. Page 83, Brooklyn Museum / Wikimedia Commons. Page 85.1, Massachusetts Bible Society. Page 88, Renata Sedmakova / Shutterstock.

Chapter 6: Page 92, AmerikoV / Wikimedia Commons. Page 94, Brooklyn Museum / Wikimedia Commons. Page 98, Ira and Larry Goldberg. Page 100.1 Everett Collection / Shutterstock. Page 100.2, Classical Numismatic Group. Page 101, Classical Numismatic Group. Page 103.2, Renata Sedmakova / Shutterstock. Page 104, ruskpp / Shutterstock. Page 107, Zvonimir Atletic / Shutterstock.

Chapter 7: Page 110, public domain / Wikimedia Commons. Page 113, Metropolitan Museum of Art / Wikimedia Commons. Page 116.1, public domain / Wikimedia Commons. Page 117, public domain / Wikimedia Commons. Page 121.2, public domain / Wikimedia Commons. Page 122, Brooklyn Museum / Wikimedia Commons. Page 125, Freedom Studio / Shutterstock.

Chapter 8: Page 130.2, public domain / Wikimedia Commons. Page 132, WolfgangRieger / Wikimedia Commons. Page 136, Moti Meiri / Shutterstock.

Chapter 9: Page 138, Morphart Creation / Shutterstock. Page 141.1, Sodabottle / Wikimedia Commons. Page 142.2, public domain / Wikimedia Commons. Page 145, public domain / Wikimedia Commons. Page 146, udi Steinwell / Wikimedia Commons. Page 148.3,Carole Raddato / Wikimedia Commons. Page 151, Sergey Kohl / Shutterstock. Page 152, Metropolitan Museum of Art / Wikimedia Commons. Page 154, Renata Sedmakova / Shutterstock. Page 157, John S.C. Abbott / Wikimedia Commons. Page 159, public domain / Wikimedia Commons. Page 162.1, Bibliothèque Nationale de France / Wikimedia Commons. Page 162.2, Michel Bakni / Wikimedia Commons. Page 167.1, gill_penney / Wikimedia Commons. Page 167.2, G.dallorto / Wikimedia Commons. Page 169, Michel Bakni / Wikimedia Commons. Page 171, Tzim78 / Wikimedia Commons. Page 172.1, public domain / Wikimedia Commons. Page 173.2, public domain / Wikimedia Commons.

Appendix A: Page 176, Mbzt / Wikimedia Commons. Page 178.2, Osama Shukir Muhammed Amin FRCP / Wikimedia Commons. Page 179.1, McKaby / Wikimedia Commons. Page 179.2, Oren Rozen / Wikimedia Commons.

Appendix B: Page180, IdoKalish / Shutterstock.

Index